AUM

THE MOMENT THAT HOLDS EVERYTHING

BY

CRAIG REUTER

DRIFT & FOG PRESS

Published by Drift & Fog Press

ISBN 979-8-218-89113-8

Cover by Anze Ban Virant - ABV Atelier Design

First Edition

Printed in the United States of America

For Prudence—
my anchor, my softness,
my quiet lesson.

Thank you in all the ways you will never know.

Note to the Reader

If you're holding this book, there's a good chance your mind has been louder than you'd like for longer than feels reasonable. Not broken. Not failing. Just tired in that particular way that comes from thinking too much for too many years. I wrote this for people who know that kind of tiredness well.

Nothing here asks you to believe in anything. You don't need a spiritual background, a philosophy degree, or a specific posture, breath technique, or wardrobe. Meditation, as I've learned it, doesn't require chanting, robes, or personality upgrades. It simply meets you where you already are: a person with a mind that occasionally becomes too much.

I didn't come to meditation through mysticism or retreat centers. I came to it because my thoughts wouldn't leave me alone. My mind narrated, worried, compared, predicted, replayed—often before I even opened my eyes for the day. If your mind does something similar, then we're starting from the same place. I'm not writing this from a mountaintop. I'm writing it from an ordinary life, trying to understand the noise the same way everyone else does.

I mention the Western mind because it's the only one I've lived inside. I can't speak for other cultures with any authority. The patterns I describe are the ones I've seen in myself and in the people around me. Some may feel familiar to you; others may not. Take what resonates and ignore the rest. This isn't a universal map—it's one person's attempt to make sense of his own thinking.

Before going any further, one idea might be useful: nothing in this book is true or false in any absolute way. Everything I describe is simply how things look through my lens. Your own lens will show something different—because that's what lenses do. They reveal from their angle. There's no single correct view here. Only perspectives.

And while meditation may sound impossibly out of reach, it works more like a skill than a revelation. If you told me I could one day do a backflip, I'd laugh. My athletic career began and ended with "stop, drop, and roll." But most people could learn a backflip with enough time, discipline, and decent instruction. Watching the Olympics is breathtaking, but gymnasts aren't gods—they're humans who practiced something intentionally. Meditation is the same. Just as every body contains the potential to become a world-class athlete, every mind contains the potential to become a working-class meditator—someone who shows up, practices in small, consistent ways, and benefits from the effort.

My hope for you is simple: that somewhere in these pages, something helps you meet your mind with a little more room and a little less struggle. That you find even one moment of quiet in a life that rarely offers many. If that happens—even once—that's enough for me

Aum

What is before me

occupies the space within.

Is this what I am?

Most people don't seek meditation because they want enlightenment. They seek it because something inside them has begun to slip in ways they cannot name. Not dramatically, not with the spectacle of a breakdown, but with the quiet erosion that happens after years of moving from one obligation to the next. A fading. A thinning. A sense that the part of them that used to feel alive is now hidden behind a fog they keep meaning to walk through but never quite reach. Meditation becomes not a spiritual ambition but a private admission: I can't keep living like this.

And yet the moment we try to be still, we discover how unfamiliar stillness has become. The body fidgets. The mind swings wildly. Thoughts scatter like startled birds. The whole interior world floods the moment as if it has been waiting just behind a door we rarely open. The first instinct is always self-doubt: *Why is my mind like this? Why can't I do something as simple as sit still? What is wrong with me?*

Nothing is wrong.

This is simply the first time you've heard your mind without the noise of living drowning it out.

Meditation does not create chaos; it reveals it. It shows you the backlog you carry, the tension you never feel until you stop, the undercurrent of thought running beneath the entire architecture of your life. When you remove distraction, you don't find peace — you find honesty. And honesty, at first, can feel unbearable.

But beneath the noise, the mind has a structure. Thoughts arise, swirl, clash, dissolve. Some come heated. Some come soft. Many repeat themselves like a skipping record. The inner narrator — that voice that comments, critiques, rehearses, keeps score — suddenly appears in full volume. Most people never realize how loud that voice has become until silence is attempted.

Yet even inside the noise, there are moments — tiny, delicate, easily missed — where the narrator goes quiet. A breath where thought loosens. A moment where awareness stands without commentary.

You've tasted this before.

Everyone has.

The pause before sleep claims you.

The moment sunlight hits dust in the air.

A stretch of shoreline where you forget yourself for half a second.

The sound of someone breathing in the dark.

2

The quiet right after laughter.

Those brief, ungraspable instants where you catch life without your mind telling you what it means.

That is aum.

Aum is not a chant. Not a symbol. Not a mystical vibration.

Aum is the instant the narrator forgets to speak.

Presence before you name it.

Awareness before you interpret it.

You, before the idea of you arrives to explain things.

Aum is subtle, but it is real — the smallest doorway into the self that isn't built from stories, judgments, memories, or fears. It is the mind resting in its natural state: untouched, unguided, unedited.

Meditation begins when we learn to recognize these moments.

And recognition changes everything.

Because once you taste awareness without narration, you begin to understand that thoughts are not commands, emotions are not dictators, and the restless machinery inside you is not the truth of you. The mind produces weather; awareness observes it. As they say, the storms do not define the sky.

Think of thoughts the way you might watch birds crossing a field. Some glide low, some soar high, some land briefly, some vanish as quickly as they appear. You don't chase them or shout instructions. You simply witness their motion. Thoughts are no different. They migrate, linger, lift off again. They do not require obedience — only observation.

This is the quiet power of aum.

Not silence, but separation.

Not control, but clarity.

You begin to see that the mind's movements are natural.

And more importantly: you are not those movements.

The sense of self we defend so fiercely shifts from moment to moment. It is not a fixed identity but a moving configuration. Beliefs change. Moods change. Desires flicker. Attachments loosen or tighten depending on the hour. The "you" of this morning is not the same "you" who will read these pages tonight.

Meditation does not create this truth — it reveals it.

Aum lets you feel it.

At first, this can be unsettling. We want to be solid. We want the self to be one shape, not a shifting constellation of impressions and reactions. But the more you sit, the more you notice the fluidity of your inner life: thoughts sliding into each other, feelings blooming and dissolving, the mind changing direction without warning. You realize you are not a fixed point at all — you are movement, and always have been.

Meditation is the art of noticing that movement without panicking.

Aum is the soft landing inside that noticing.

As the mind becomes more familiar, something unexpected happens. The moments of aum stop feeling accidental. They lengthen. First a breath, then two. Then, without realizing it, you find yourself resting in awareness rather than being pulled by thought. You begin to sense a space in you that does not collapse under emotion — a space the mind cannot chatter over, a space that feels like you without the story of you.

This space is not fragile.

It survives you.

It survives your fear.

It survives your grief.

It survives your overthinking.

It survives every storm the mind throws.

Most people spend their lives fighting the contents of their mind rather than noticing the awareness in which those contents appear. Aum is the beginning of that noticing — a pinprick of light in the fabric of thought. Once you see it, your relationship with your mind shifts forever.

Meditation does not demand that you empty the mind.

That is not possible.

Nor does it ask you to transcend yourself or abandon your humanity.

It asks only that you stop running long enough to see how much motion you carry — to feel the truth you spend most of your life avoiding: that nothing in you is still.

Not your thoughts.

Not your emotions.

Not your sense of self.

Not even your awareness.

You are a river pretending to be a rock.

The beginning of meditation is realizing that the pretending is optional.

As you continue on this path, the mind becomes less something to conquer and more something to understand. You begin to see how it tries to protect you — how it anticipates danger, clings to patterns that once kept you safe, pushes away what it fears, grasps at what it craves. How it exhausts itself trying to hold together a self that keeps shifting beneath it.

Aum does not dismantle the self; it simply introduces you to the part of you that is not frightened by its instability. The part that can watch without tightening. The part that remains when everything else is in motion.

That is where this chapter leaves you:
standing in the truth that you are already in flux.
Your mind is moving.
Your identity is moving.
Your inner world is moving.
And the path ahead is not about forcing stillness — it is about learning to remain awake inside this motion.

In the next chapter, we will look outward, into the world that shaped this motion — the culture that taught you to sprint, the expectations that drained you, the noise that drowned your longing.

But before we confront the world outside, you must see what is happening inside.
You are not a fixed self.
You are a shifting one.
And meditation begins here,
in the quiet recognition
that nothing in you has ever been still.

Oh, How the West Has Won

I pass through myself

like weather crossing a field—

then linger, surprised.

Life is movement. Everything changes. The mind, the body, the people we love, the stories we tell ourselves—all of it shifting in ways we rarely acknowledge until something forces us to pause. In the last chapter, I ended with the idea that we are living in flux whether we want to or not. The work ahead is not to escape the movement, but to stay awake inside it.

But there is another layer to this, one we must face before anything meaningful can begin.

We were not raised to understand our own minds.

We were raised to outrun them.

The confusion we feel when we first try to sit with ourselves isn't a personal failure. It has roots—cultural, inherited expectations, a lifetime of being trained to move faster than our inner life can follow. We're taught how to produce, compete, anticipate, adjust. But almost no one teaches us how to rest. How to listen. How to exist without performing.

So when the mind begins to reveal its noise, we blame ourselves. But the truth is far simpler and far harder: we have been shaped by a world that leaves very little room for inner life at all.

This shows up first as fatigue. Then numbness. Then the quiet dread of a person who has been in motion too long. Somewhere along the way, we learn to survive instead of live, and we don't realize the transformation until long after it has completed itself.

We live in a loop.

Alarm.

Second alarm.

Third alarm.

The sound drills into the skull like paperwork being stamped in some distant, indifferent office.

You rise because the body obeys before the mind consents, you rise because it's more comfortable than being still.

Wash face.

Brush teeth.

The mirror shows a person you vaguely remember applying for this position.

Then traffic—lines of metal coffins crawling toward obligations no one recalls agreeing to.

Work.

Work.

Work.

Hours vanish into screens and forms and tasks whose meaning evaporated years ago, but whose inertia remains. You answer emails like a clerk stamping documents that will never be read. You perform, not because it matters, but because stopping would require explaining yourself to a system that has never once acknowledged you.

Lunch isn't lunch.

It's refueling the machine you drag around.

Then sitting.

Staring.

Keyboards rattling like insect wings in an office hive.

The air smells faintly of plastic and resignation.

More work.

More tasks multiplying in the inbox like vermin.

Then traffic again—the same red lights, the same exhaust, the same quiet suspicion that you died sometime back in your twenties and nobody had the courtesy to notify you.

Home.

Collapse.

Scroll.

Blank faces in rectangles.

Bodies performing happiness.

Vacations. Meals. Upward trajectories.

Tiny glowing windows pressing into your retinas until your thoughts dissolve into static.

Your apartment becomes another waiting room.

Another holding pen.

Another place where nothing happens, but everything demands your attention anyway.

Then insomnia.

Not dramatic, but punitive.

The ceiling becomes an interrogation lamp.

The silence turns into a question you cannot answer.

Thoughts sprout legs and burrow into the chest, writhing behind the sternum.

Breath thins.

Time thickens.

You lie there in a body that feels borrowed, wondering when the lease runs out.

Then alarm.

Second alarm.

Third alarm.

As if the universe keeps insisting you re-enter a life you can barely inhabit.

We do not live in America.

We endure it—defendants in a trial where no charges are listed, only sentences.

Inside all of this, something begins to stir.

Not panic.

Not hope.

Something older.

A small Buddha, curled in the center of your being, taps once against your temple.

Not forceful—patient.

A reminder that something essential has been misplaced.

Something that belonged to you before the world drafted you into its bureaucracy.

We try to drown it out with distractions, vices, fantasies, one-click shopping.

But it persists, the way truth persists when ignored: quietly, relentlessly, waiting for a crack in the noise.

Meanwhile, outside: the insult of order.

Deer step out at dusk, always on time.

The moon climbs with absolute confidence, never behind schedule.

The tide breathes in. The tide breathes out. Never anxious, never late.

The sun rises each morning as if it remembers what we've forgotten.

Everything outside moves with ancient precision.

Everything inside shudders like a filing cabinet forced shut over the years.

And it was in the middle of that—inside the dizziness, the absurdity, the mechanized days stacked like outdated forms— that I found myself brushing my teeth one morning, staring into the mirror, and saying aloud to no one:

I should want to be joyous.

For a moment, everything stopped.

The electric hum of the bathroom light.

The rush in my ears.

The suffocating momentum of the morning.

All of it paused, as though the world itself exhaled with me. I stood there, toothbrush in hand, suspended between the life I had been enduring and the faint possibility of one I had not yet remembered to want.

If one desires anything at all, the Buddha said, let it be the desire to awaken.

The strange part was not the sentence itself but the realization hiding inside it:

I should *want* to be joyous.

Not that I should be joyous.

Not that joy was missing.

Not that I had fallen out of some radiant state and needed to claw my way back in.

It was that the desire for joy had gone quiet somewhere along the way—replaced by habit and fatigue and the mechanical rhythm of a life that demanded movement without direction. It was the wanting that had died first, and I had been too busy to notice.

The truth of it sat in the mirror like something I had been avoiding for years. I had not forgotten how to feel joy. I had forgotten that I was allowed to reach for it. And somewhere between the alarms and the traffic and the dull ache behind my eyes, I had stopped believing that joy was something I deserved to want in the first place.

That is a different kind of loss.

A quieter one.

The sort that does not announce itself with collapse or crisis, but slowly seeps into the corners of a life until one day you're brushing your teeth and telling the mirror that you should want to be joyous.

And that moment, small as it was, became a turning point. A hinge. An admission that the life I had been living was not a life at all but a carefully managed sequence of responsibilities and distractions. It was a system that kept me upright but never awake.

It is one thing to say I want to be happy.

It is another to confess that you no longer know how to want happiness at all.

That confession is the real beginning.

It is where meditation stops being a practice and becomes a necessity.

It is where silence becomes medicine.

It is where stillness becomes the only honest place to stand.

Every seeker begins not with enlightenment but with the admission that something essential has slipped away, and for me, it began with those six words in the mirror:

I should want to be joyous.

I didn't understand why the desire for joy had gone quiet. Not then. I only felt the absence, the hollowness where longing used to live. But absences have origins. Silences have ancestry. Something in me had been thinning for years, worn down not by catastrophe but by a thousand small distractions pulling in opposite directions.

The moment wasn't an epiphany. It was the first crack. And through that crack, I began to notice the shape of the life that had been living me. The noise. The drift. The slow siphoning of attention so constant I had mistaken it for my own personality.

Before meditation could begin, I had to see what had been feeding on the space where awareness should have lived.

The Feed That Feeds on Us

Noise repeats its noise.

Silence remembers my name.

I walk back to me.

1

There is a rhythm to modern life that isn't our heartbeat, yet carries us day by day. A choreography of reaching, checking, swiping, scrolling. Before thought can even clear its throat, the phone lifts itself into our hand like a pet that has learned our weaknesses. *Hush — don't think; don't question.* The world has become something we witness through glass. Nature replaced by notifications, sunrise replaced by a glow. We drift across streams of data as though they were rivers, moving through life with strides measured in thumb-lengths.

Algorithms tug us gently but relentlessly by the collar — just enough tension, just enough release — the way a casino circulates oxygen through its vents to keep gamblers vertical.

It is everywhere we are. As we drive, eat, wait in line, half-listen to a friend — our bodies perform their ancient roles while our minds orbit elsewhere. Life becomes something we attend to in the margins. Every post, notification, and message informs us of what we should feel, think, desire. We no longer search for longing or cultivate it; we simply download a facsimile.

It is one of the reasons, I suspect, that I lost my desire to want. Years of instant, continuous stimulation create dopamine-driven minds that have forgotten how to wait. The feed keeps us content enough — not genuinely satisfied, but docile. Contentment replaces joy, and because joy demands the full orchestration of inner life, we gradually forget the steps. Beautiful moments still happen, but they no longer detonate inside us the way they once did.

We do not feel less because life became shallow. We feel less because we did.

We learned connection without presence, communication without voice, stimulation without intimacy. And the mind — clever animal that it is — learned to distance from itself to keep pace. The body wants rhythm, breath, continuity. The scroll wants speed, novelty, splintering.

2

What has changed is the tempo — the speed from event to event, distraction to distraction. We do not wake into our lives;

we wake into the backlog. Into the catching-up-on. The eyes
open and immediately fill with distant tragedies, curated joys,
and fictional lives that make ours seem dull by comparison.
And it happens fast — faster than the psyche can defend itself
— until movement feels pointless and meaning feels like
something that requires a username and password.

Plutarch once wrote that the mind resembles a city:
crowded, bright, exhausting. But even ancient cities slept. Ours
doesn't. It stays awake on a six-inch slab of glass that promises
connection, delivering distraction. Like cotton candy: exquisite
for a moment, nutritionally vacant forever.

Neither phone nor media is the villain. The problem is
reliance — the constant leaning on stimulation to feel anything
at all. We are restless, anxious, easily bored, and discomforted
by the mere idea of nothing happening. Stillness has become
foreign. Silence, suspicious. Depth, something to be filled with
someone else's inspirational quote.

Presence has worn thin. You can see through it if you hold
it up to the light.

3

The infinite scroll survives because it offers the illusion of
continuity while delivering nothing conclusive. We lean
toward a future moment the feed promises but never provides.
It is the inverse of nature: seeds ripen to fruit, rivers dry,
chords resolve — but the feed opens door after identical door,
nothing beyond but more hallways.

This endless forward-tilt exhausts the psyche. No wonder
half the Western world lives with their shoulders touching

ears. The body braces for something unclear because the scroll never announces arrival. Only "maybe soon."

Meditation reverses the direction. Instead of leaning toward the next moment, awareness sinks into this one. The breath's cadence. The heft of the chest. The trembling quiet behind the lips. Once you actually notice these things, it becomes harder to fall for the idea that life is elsewhere.

Meditation teaches you to scroll without drowning, engage without dissolving, use the tool without becoming its architecture.

Intermittent reinforcement — unpredictable rewards — fuels the scroll's power. Sometimes a post delights, sometimes it wounds, sometimes it does both in five seconds. The unpredictability hooks us; the nervous system stays invested because it might get something meaningful.

Meanwhile, inner life is neglected. Rooms within us gather dust. We forget where the light switches are.

Meditation reopens the house. It prepares the rooms for you to rest in again.

4

But as inner spaces go, we do not enter them willingly. Forget your phone at home and your entire nervous system files a complaint. Hands twitch. Neck swivels in confusion. Your senses, deprived of digital anesthesia, finally register the world — slow, quiet, indifferent to your panic.

Meditation teaches the mind to witness itself in relation to the frantic pace of modern life. Rather than being carried by chaos, you watch it pass like a parade. One breath at a time, authority returns. Attention becomes something you can place, not something being stolen.

It restores the thread of continuity. It repairs the "I" that gets lost when the mind is dragged through a thousand micro-identities in ten minutes. It is not dramatic. It is remembering you had a body before someone convinced you to live only from the eyes out.

5

One day, something shifts. Nothing in the world changes. Your apps still sit where you left them, the notifications still vie for your attention. Everything outside remains the same. The shift happens in you. You notice the scroll isn't happening inside you anymore. It's happening "over there," at a distance, almost like watching play from the mezzanine. The feed is still moving, but it's no longer moving you. That small separation is the first subtle sign of transformation.

Presence starts to feel natural again. Stillness stops feeling like a prison you need to escape. Attention becomes intention you set, instead of something that is taken away. You realize the change isn't external; it's entirely internal. The world didn't quiet down, you did. You scroll, but the scroll no longer scrolls you. You feel the impulse to reach for your phone, but now you also feel the space around that impulse. And inside that small gap, choice appears. That gap is the beginning of awareness. It's where sovereignty starts.

Meditation doesn't create that gap; it reveals it. And once it's revealed, you begin noticing things you used to rush past without a second thought. The details stop disappearing into the background. They register. Life stops feeling skimmed and starts feeling inhabited.

The feed becomes a tool rather than a habitat — something you visit, not a place you live. It stops dictating your mood, your pace, your sense of urgency. Silence no longer feels like deprivation; it feels like room to think. Your body stops bracing. Your mind stops grasping. Your breath stops apologizing for existing.

Nothing changed. The internal merely shifted from hunger to awareness, and awareness changes everything. Modern life pushes you toward broken attention. Meditation offers a counterproposal: attention returned to itself. When attention becomes whole, so do you. And from that steadiness, the next step becomes possible — turning inward and seeing the mind as it actually is.

Which is exactly where the next chapter begins.

The Mind's Illusions

The self bends like light

shaped by windows of the mind.

Nothing stands alone.

You do not realize how much of your life has been lived for you until stillness turns toward you and reveals the scaffolding the mind has built in your absence. You begin noticing the structures you inherited rather than chose: the thoughts that echo voices long gone, the reflexes shaped by old hurts or childhood misunderstandings, the narrations that run on their own momentum. You have been nodding along to a voice you assumed was yours simply because you never turned around to see who was speaking.

Meditation lifts this curtain slowly. The boundaries of what you call "I" begin to soften, the edges flicker, and you sense that the self you defend so fiercely is less a single thing than a legion of unexamined impulses negotiating under one name. In this shift, a line from *Don Juan* lands with unusual clarity: "Nobody knows who I am or what I do. Not even I".

Not mysticism—just honesty about the way awareness disassembles its own story when given the space.

To encounter the self through meditation, remember that it is a device whose craft is not honed quickly. People say they "cannot meditate" in the same tone they admit they cannot draw or sing, but meditation is not performance. It is a tool. A hammer does not ask for genius, only a hand willing to try. And like any tool, meditation feels clumsy at first. Thoughts spill everywhere. The mind wanders. Restlessness rises. This is not failure. This is the sound of a long-neglected space being opened for the first time.

The confusion of the beginner is not a flaw. It is the initiation.

Language betrays us here. We say "I meditated" as though the action originated in our effort alone, but meditation is less an act than an arrangement. You place your attention a certain way and let the mind reveal itself. A carpenter does not blame the hammer when he bends a few nails; he simply grows steadier with the tool. The same is true when you begin turning your awareness inward.

Teaching works the same way. Some minds learn through sound, some through reading, some through touch, some through failure. Meditation has no single doorway. It has a thousand. Posture is not sacred. Breath is not sacred. Technique is not sacred. What is sacred is the understanding these methods lead you toward—the recognition of what remains when the mind stops interpreting everything it encounters.

Understanding seldom appears in the objects themselves. It rises in the space between them: the pauses, the silences, the

21

intervals. Meditation teaches you to sense the gaps instead of grasping the things that surround them, to feel the cadence of a page by noticing the stillness between the words.

Ordinary thinking cannot enter this place because ordinary thinking is always about something—memory, plan, threat, injury. The mind leaps from object to object as though the spaces between them are dangerous pitfalls. But you already know how to think without words. You know it every time you hum a melody you've never heard, every time your fingers drift toward a texture that draws you before you name it, every time you sit in sunlight and feel warmth without generating a story about the moment.

Meditation teaches you to trust those wordless moments.

And then, slowly, it invites you toward nothingness—not absence, but unfilled presence. To meditate on nothingness is to stop clinging to something-ness. The mind resists this because it has spent its entire life fastening itself to objects, labels, expectations, interpretations—anything to avoid the terror of being without a story. But when you loosen the story, you discover the space beneath it is not empty. It is simply wider than the mind can comfortably hold.

There is the world of things—solid, measurable, nameable. And there is the world beneath that world: the unformed, the uncreated, the invisible conditions from which everything rises. These are not separate realms but two ways of seeing the same one, the way a landscape feels utterly different at dawn and at noon though the land itself has not changed—only the light.

You stand at the seam of these two perspectives. Uneasy with uncertainty, the mind draws boundaries: this is me, that is not; this is real, that is imagined. But these boundaries are habits, not truth.

Consider the senses you do not have: the dog who reads histories from a scent; the bird who feels north the way you feel a shift of wind; the viper who perceives heat as shape. Yet we insist our narrow slice defines reality. We behave like fish convinced water covers the entire universe simply because it covers theirs.

Meditation softens this certainty. When stimulation fades, the mind rushes to fill the blank with memory or fantasy or fear. It would rather invent a world than sit quietly in one that has not yet become something. In the quiet beneath that invention, the vibration of aum returns—not as sound but as sensation, the hum beneath interference, the tone of being before the mind tightens around it.

Consider the earliest stage of life: a fetus drifting in warm darkness, sensing only pressure, pulse, enclosure. Then one day the mother enters sunlight and a wash of rose glow slips inward. No concept. No comparison. The universe expands. Later come muffled vibrations of voices and heartbeats. They mean nothing, yet shape everything. Experience precedes comprehension. Presence precedes thought. Meditation leads you back there.

This is why flutes, howls, and chants feel transformative. They slip beneath interpretation. They speak a proto-language. The sound does not pass through you; it happens within you. For a moment the edges of the self thin, and something in you remembers.

As stillness deepens, the boundary between observer and observed loosens. You are not the one looking at the world; you are the place where the world appears. You are not adrift in space; space is held within you. Walt Whitman understood this when he wrote that he contained multitudes — describing not ego, but the dissolving of ego, the expansion of the self into the field that holds all experience.

This dissolving leads to what older traditions called maya, a word often flattened into "illusion" but describing something more intimate: the world shaped by the mind that looks at it.

For some people maya is an idea. For others, a recognition: that reality is always slightly unstable at the edges. I learned this long ago and inked the word down the back of my neck where I cannot see it but always feel it. Fitting — illusion resting just out of sight, influencing everything without entering view. A private truth, hidden openly.

Maya is easily understood through the metaphor of a hall of mirrors: everywhere you turn, a version of you. Some flattering. Some unsettling. Some unrecognizable. In so many reflections, you forget none are original — if an original exists at all. The mind does this constantly. It reflects the world in shapes of its own making, and you mistake reflection for reality.

Meditation does not shatter the mirrors. It simply reveals that they are mirrors.

And the deeper you look, the more you see how the mind invents what it cannot confirm, how it fills empty spaces with fragments of old stories, how perception mutates with context. A car passing on your street becomes a threat in a dark forest — the same input, a different meaning — because meaning is constructed, not delivered. Meditation shows how often that construction replaces the world without your consent and without leaving a trace.

24

When you sit long enough to sense the body without the old hierarchy, you discover that awareness is not perched behind the eyes. The toe is as present as the forehead; the spine as present as the breath. The small narrator dissolves. The body becomes a field rather than a location. You inhabit yourself differently—wholly—without a center.

This is not disorientation. This is the beginning of clarity.

Meditation does not remove the mind. It illuminates it. You begin seeing how much suffering came from believing every thought as if it were a verdict. When you loosen your grip on thought—when you allow space around what hurts—the world softens. The edges of experience gain breath. The life you have always lived feels less like something collapsing upon you and more like something unfolding through you.

Meditation gives you that space—not to escape or deny—but to stop demanding that reality explain itself before you allow yourself to inhabit it.

You do not meditate to become someone else.

You meditate to stop letting the mind choose your life for you.

Because the world will keep being the world, and the mind will keep being the mind—but you do not have to suffer both at the same time.

You meditate to feel what is real before the mind names it.

The Moment Is All

A soft light widens.

I forget where I begin—

and breathe without name.

1

The mind is a peculiar thing. It shows itself only when we stop trying to control it. *I do not want the worst of me to get the best of us.* That is the quiet risk in every relationship, inner or outer. There is a part of us that hurts, that fears, that retreats, always waiting for the moment when fatigue makes us careless. And when the worst in us rises, it doesn't come alone. It drags with it the world that shaped it.

And that world was never built on independence. We like to imagine we stand on our own, but nothing stands alone. We are, and have always been, in dependence—reliant on history, on habit, on the thousand invisible hands that molded our reflexes long before we noticed we had any. If you doubt this, walk on no ground and see how far you get.

Everything leans. Everything inherits. And when ascending the mountain feels impossible, look closely: often it is the mountain descending beneath your feet that is doing the shaping. And because so much of us is built from what we never chose, the distortions we carry do not feel foreign. They feel like "me."

This is why the body of lies we tell ourselves grows so quietly. It stretches from the crown of the head to the soles of the feet, filling the narrow interior corridor where truth ought to breathe. Expectations, cultural mandates, inherited philosophies, old fears rising from the dark ocean within—all of it saturating the self until its weight masquerades as identity. We are born into a suffering world and emerge shaped by it, taught to see ourselves in binaries: too much or not enough, success or failure, worthy or wanting. Rules, laws, norms, customs—these carve us into shapes that fit easily but were never designed for the person actually living inside them.

What informs the mind is not what forms the mind. The eyes are not the center of us. They are windows, not a throne. My central self is no more behind my eyes than it is in the far edge of my toe. When I close my eyes and stop pretending that I am still seeing, something begins to widen. The sense of self expands in all directions, though without a frame of reference I cannot tell how far. It could be inches. It could be eons.

At the edges of this expanded self, you may feel the bed beneath you, the pressure of gravity, the movement of heat or cold. If someone were to tap your shoulder, it would feel like a rap against the hull of a spacecraft. Something inside knows we are not the sensations pressed against us. We are the one who notices them. Bound and shaped by the world, dependent on it, leaning into it the way any new life leans into the one that first held it.

It is easy to forget this dependence. Easy to imagine ourselves as isolated, self-contained, separate. Easy to dismiss a grain of sand in a distant galaxy or an ex-spouse as irrelevant. But this is not a philosophy of physics or destiny. This is a way of arriving where we must go. If we reach the destination, the path will only prove itself.

We must recognize that the self suffers. And it suffers with everyone else. I am hurt by your suffering, and you are hurt by mine. We are entangled—not metaphorically, but experientially. Whatever game we inherited, it is making everyone miserable. So the question becomes simple: what is the exit strategy?

The exit is not to end suffering. That is beyond us. The exit is to not suffer our suffering.

Which brings us to this perplexing mind, that persistent witness threading through every moment of experience. The body is rigid and linear, confined to place, but the mind moves like a pendulum, swinging between then and when, rarely touching the now. It can occupy memories and futures simultaneously. It can scatter itself across imagined risks, replayed conversations, and scenarios that have never happened and never will. It oscillates around the present, analyzing, correcting, protecting—constantly evaluating whether our choices were good, whether we are safe, whether we are prepared for what comes next.

And then, when we finally become immersed in the present, the mind spirals open like a vortex, witnessing everything happening everywhere, no longer a pendulum but a widening circle.

This is where meditation becomes essential, because until we learn to steady the mind, we cannot stop suffering our suffering.

Meditation is not an escape from the mind. It is the first honest meeting with it. There is a common belief that meditation quiets thoughts, but silence is not the starting point. Silence is a consequence. The starting point is witnessing the chaos we live inside every moment of the day yet almost never acknowledge. When we sit — when we stop moving, when we stop distracting ourselves — the mind does not settle. It flares. It fills the room. It rushes into the newly opened space like water through a broken hull.

The irritation, the restlessness, the discomfort — these are not failures of meditation. They are introductions. They are the self saying, *this is what I have been carrying while you were busy. This is the backlog of your life. This is the suffering you have been suffering without knowing it.* You are meeting the weight you refused to feel.

Most people interpret this as a sign they are bad at meditation. They quit after a few attempts, believing they lack the temperament or discipline or spiritual purity. But meditation is not about purity. It is the opposite. It is the practice of becoming aware of the impurities — the distortions, the tensions, the pressures — and learning to sit with them until they begin to soften. It is the wiping away of dust from a most precious jewel.

Before anything becomes profound, it must become simple. Meditation is no different. You don't begin with depth or discipline; you begin with willingness. Think *Charlotte's Web*, not Chaucer. No one learns to read by wrestling with Middle English. You begin with something warm, familiar, human. Your mind deserves the same grace. So for now, forget the mystical ideas, the elaborate postures, the impossible stillness. We're just taking the mind by the hand and letting it settle for a moment.

Like a flashlight, the mind has been taught to look in every direction except inward. It has been conditioned to anticipate danger, replay mistakes, plan contingencies, and fill silence with commentary. Sitting still does not feel natural because we have never been taught that stillness is allowed. We know how to work. We know how to endure. We know how to produce, to perform, to persevere. We do not know how to be.

Meditation teaches being. Not as a mystical state, but as a biological one.

The nervous system has rhythms as ancient as tides and winds, and they are not aligned with the culture we have built. The body wants to breathe deeply. The mind wants to rest. The emotions want space to unwind. The faithfulness of deer and moon and tide is inside us too, but we have forgotten how to feel it.

Any true feeling of peace or comfort or happiness must occur in the present moment. Music is one of the simplest places to see this, because you cannot experience a song outside of the now. You cannot dance ahead of the beat, and you cannot listen to a melody that has not yet arrived. The moment leads and you follow. Alan Watts admitted this was the secret: the journey is not toward the dance; the dance itself is the point. Music teaches presence without ever announcing itself as teacher. It pulls you along one note at a time, grounding you in the unfolding of the moment, and for a little while the mind forgets to wander.

When you are inside a piece of music, you cannot dance with anger. You cannot rehearse old arguments. You cannot project yourself into the future. The song does not allow it. What is outside the music becomes irrelevant, because the music is always being played in the only place anything real can be played: here. Now. The beat becomes a kind of harbor, a refuge from the mind's restless motion, and without even knowing it you enter a moment of aum—not the mystical form you read about in old texts, but the simple aum of being where your life is actually happening.

Meditation is no different. It is the same principle without the melody. It is the discipline of staying with the cadence of each moment as it arrives without reaching ahead for the next one. It is listening without trying to predict the chorus. It is being danced by your own breath.

And then, when the mind begins to steady—even for a few seconds—something remarkable happens. The pendulum slows. The vortex expands without swallowing us. The self becomes less confined to a point behind the eyes and begins to distribute its presence throughout the body. There is a sense of occupying the whole form, a sense of resting inside one's own life instead of bracing against it.

This widening is the threshold. And it is here something extraordinary once happened to me.

2

There was a moment once, years before I understood any of this, when the mind slipped out of its usual shape and something uncommon occurred. I was in a yoga class, lying on my back, listening to my teacher guide the room through a slow, rhythmic breath. Nothing felt special. My body was tight, my thoughts restless, my attention stubbornly ordinary.

And then, without warning, the commentary stopped. Not because I silenced it. Not because I tried. One moment the mind was full. The next, it was not.

In its place was not silence so much as absence—the absence of "me." No inner narrator. No identity. No body on a mat. No memory of myself or awareness of my surroundings. Just awareness, unattached to anyone.

And in that awareness: a cardinal. Perched on a snow-covered branch. Winter light bending around it. The red of its feathers startling in its clarity. The scene was not recalled or imagined. It did not feel symbolic. It was simply happening.

There was no sense of *I am seeing this*. There was only the seeing.

Then the bird moved its head, and the moment shifted again. A horse appeared with its breath fogging in the air. Then the sky widened into galaxies, distances without measure. Not visions. Not fantasies. Experience without a center.

Then my teacher's voice entered: *when you're ready, begin returning to the room.*

And I fell instantly back into myself—with body, heat, breath, ceiling lights, the weight of being someone again. For a second I felt disoriented, as though I had stepped through the wrong door in my own mind.

This was not a trance or a hallucination. I was not dreaming, nor was I unconscious. The mind did not fabricate images; it simply stopped filtering experience through the usual sense of "me." Whether they arose from memory, imagination, or some deeper perceptual layer is not the point. What matters was the mode of awareness: clean, unhindered, without commentary or identity. The dissolution yielded to the saturation of the mind—how vivid and complete thoughts can be when given room to breathe.

Dreams are this way as well. Freed of lucidity or sense of self, we drift into all sorts of wild adventures whose fidelity can stand in for reality. Experiences like this are uncommon, and they are not the goal of meditation. The reader is not expected to seek them, replicate them, or desire them. They are simply what can happen when the inner narrator steps aside for a moment and the mind returns to its bare capacity to perceive.

What stayed with me was not the imagery. It was the understanding that followed. Awareness remains even when the self dissolves. Perception continues even without a narrator. The mind can function more clearly when it is not pretending to be someone.

I did not cause that moment. I could not force it to happen again. But it showed me that aum is not theoretical. It is not mystical. It is something the mind already knows how to do when it stops clutching itself.

When the narrator loosens and the self stops bracing, something softens. Relief begins, not because suffering disappears, but because we finally occupy a part of ourselves that is not made of suffering. Thoughts can be witnessed rather than believed. Emotion can be felt without being drowned by

33

it. The mind stops running from itself long enough to remember that it was never meant to be the enemy.

The world outside will continue as it does: loud, demanding, full of alarms and obligations. But inside, the pendulum has slowed. Inside, there is a place that does not move. A place where the moment can be held without fear. A place where the weight of being someone becomes lighter.

Meditation begins here, in this fragile and unfamiliar ability to simply be with what is.

The Art of Returning

A small sound returns,

like wings brushing through silence—

and nothing resists.

There are states you enter the way you drift into a dream: quietly, without ceremony, without any awareness of transition. One moment you are here, and the next you've gone somewhere else entirely. Meditation works the same way. You slip into it not by willpower but by softness, the same way a daydream steals a few minutes from you without asking permission. Returning feels just as familiar. It's like driving several exits past your turn and only noticing once you've come back to yourself. The mind remembers itself only when it returns.

Meditation is not an escape from the world, and it is not a departure from anything real. It is only the ego that interprets stillness as absence. The part of you that signs your name, that introduces itself at social gatherings, that fills out questionnaires and résumés — that part panics at silence because it assumes silence means something is wrong. But meditation is simply the moment when you stop carrying that usual self with you. This is not the drifting of a daydream or the wandering of the night-mind. Moments of aum are quiet reunions with what has always been here beneath the surface.

When we sit to meditate, we often expect clarity, transformation, or at least a moment of relief. Instead, the mind begins projecting old films: memory, fantasy, worry, planning, regret. We assume meditation has failed. But the mind has never been quiet for more than a few seconds in your entire life. Why expect it to behave differently now?

If you read a novel and conclude "it didn't work," you would be asked what you expected it to do. Books unfold on their own terms, and so does the mind. Meditation is not something that succeeds or fails. When you meditate, you have meditated, just as when you sleep, you have slept, whether or not you dream. A thousand swings precede the first home run, yet none of those swings are failures; they are simply part of the path.

How do we begin when our ashram is a living room covered in Legos, and our inner world feels like a sports bar with every television tuned to a different anxiety? Carl Sagan once said, "If you wish to make an apple pie from scratch, you must first invent the Universe." So we begin here, exactly where we already are. You started long before you reached this page. Simply continue.

Find a position your body can inhabit without argument. The physical part of meditation begins and ends with allowing the body to be comfortable enough that it does not ask for your attention.

Before staying with the breath, let attention move through the body once.

Bring attention to the feet. Notice any sensation that is present: pressure, temperature, contact with the floor, or the absence of sensation altogether. As attention rests there, notice whether any tension softens on its own. You do not need to make this happen. The body often releases what it no longer needs once it has been noticed.

Move attention slowly upward through the lower legs, the knees, the thighs, and the hips. At each place, simply notice what is there. If tension is present, awareness may be enough for it to ease. If it does not, that is fine. Nothing is required.

Continue through the torso, noticing the points of contact beneath you and the subtle movement created by breathing. The body knows how to settle itself when it is allowed to be seen.

Let attention travel to the shoulders, the arms, and the hands. Then to the neck, the face, the jaw, the eyes, and the forehead. Finish at the top of the head. Again, notice whether areas of holding relax naturally as attention passes through, without effort or instruction.

You are not relaxing the body. You are not fixing it. You are simply noticing what is already there. Relaxation may occur. Or it may not. Both are acceptable.

If you feel nothing in an area, move on. If attention drifts, return to the next place in the body.

When the scan is complete, return to the breath.

Begin by noticing the breath. Not controlling it. Not shaping it. Just observing the slight coolness at the nostrils, the subtle lift of the chest, the faint expansion across the back. Feeling the breath is the first quiet step toward noticing.

When I first learned meditation, a Buddhist monk named Kelsang Rigpa told me to imagine a tiny camera perched on my upper lip, pointed into one nostril, watching the breath go in and out. Nothing more. And somewhere in the middle of that strange little instruction, the mind fell silent for a moment. Not dramatically. Not forever. Just for one clean second. If you find even that one second, welcome aum.

Soon the mind will rebel. It notices the quiet and immediately generates noise — thoughts, scenarios, memories, fears, arguments, fantasies. If nothing else stays with you from this book, let it be this: that is okay. This moment is where most people give up. But trying to stop the mind is like trying to stop a sneeze. It arrives regardless. Let it come.

Intrusive thoughts appear. So what. Notice them. Then return to the breath. Over and over. Not because you are failing, but because this is how the mind learns its place. Here, Albert Camus becomes unexpectedly useful; he understood the quiet rebellion of continuing despite the absurdity of things. The mind is loud. Life is loud. So what. We return anyway. Returning becomes the practice.

Meditation is not the silencing of thought or the pursuit of pristine emptiness. It is the interruption of automatic obedience. The mind thinks. Awareness notices. They are not the same. You do not need to escort thoughts anywhere, argue with them, or tidy them. You return to the breath. Eventually, the returning itself becomes the stillness you have been looking for.

As you settle deeper, you begin to sense the difference between the shallow mind and the deeper awareness beneath it. Everyday life proves this constantly: you wash dishes while thinking about next week, you drive while replaying a conversation, you shower while drafting imaginary replies. Something is always doing, and something else is always noticing.

This distinction cannot be forced. It opens naturally. Trying to separate the observer from the mind is like trying to separate water from the river. They exist together, but they are not identical. The shallow layer is the surface: fast, reactive, noisy. Beneath it is a depth that does not move with the weather.

Meditation is the act of feeling this depth without needing to explain it.

This is where certain questions begin to appear — the kind that do not seek answers but clarity. A question raised in *I Heart Huckabees*, stripped of its context but carrying the weight it deserves:

Are you being yourself?

The question exposes the gap between the persona you perform and the awareness that observes it.

And then the deeper question follows:

How am I not myself?

Once you can observe your thoughts without becoming them, you see that much of what you call "you" is simply habit. The observing part is quieter. Steadier. It does not explain itself. It notices.

This chapter has been about reaching the point where this distinction becomes clear. And now, as we close, one final image.

Imagine a sparrow. When it sings, it sings. When it does not, it does not seek silence. The sparrow does not control the song. The song arises and is permitted. The bird remains the bird.

Thoughts arise. Silence returns. Awareness remains.

Meditation is not about controlling the song.
It is about recognizing the sparrow.

Which brings us to the question, not to be answered, but to be carried:

Who sings the sparrow?

How Meditation Rewrites the Mind

A small room of breath

changes the shape of the storm—

and I step through whole.

1

For most of your life, your mind has worked in one direction: forward. Always leaning into the next task, the next responsibility, the next thing to manage. The contemporary mind is engineered for output. It plans, evaluates, rehearses, catastrophizes, strategizes, and narrates. It is a machine built on momentum, and momentum has been mistaken for intelligence.

Meditation interrupts that machinery, not by slowing it down, but by showing you how it works. You learn, for the first time, that awareness and thought are not the same thing. This is not mystical. It is practical. Once you can observe the mind instead of automatically obeying it, everything becomes less reactive. Your decision-making structure shifts quietly, almost secretly, and yet profoundly.

Most people react before they understand. Meditation teaches you to understand before you react.

This is the first and most immediate benefit of practice: awareness inserts a pause where you previously had none. The pause is not dramatic. It is a fraction of a second where the old chain of mental events breaks. That fraction of a second is the difference between spiraling or staying steady, between saying something you regret or choosing silence, between being consumed by emotion or simply noticing emotion.

It does not require a mat, a room, or a studio. Nor does it require anything that you haven't already carried since you were born. It requires only the willingness to notice.

As your practice deepens, you'll see that meditation is not something you actively pursue, but something that begins to appear in moments you once thought were unchangeable. Anger rises, and you feel the space around it. Anxiety appears, and you see it instead of becoming it. It becomes easier to notice the difference between "I am" and "I sense." A familiar irritation stirs, and for the first time you have enough distance to choose a different response. This is understanding. The mind becomes less of a tyrant and more of a tool. These changes seem small, but they accumulate. Instant reactivity gives way to deliberate response.

This is where the practice becomes useful outside the stillness. You begin noticing the places where your life once had no elasticity: the way you handle a difficult email, the way you talk to your partner, the way you read a text message that would usually set you off. You start seeing the moments where you were never actually choosing anything. This is meditation in the wild, awareness functioning in real time.

The body scan exercise was your first glimpse of this. You visited each part of your body with attention, and because you had first softened the breath, you could finally notice tensions you had been living with for years. The moment you became aware of them, they softened. Where there is unease, awareness must create a space before anything can change. The body listens and responds to the silent call of awareness.

Our culture gives no such space. We move from stress to stress, from distraction to distraction, without ever asking ourselves: *Is this okay?*

You can stand in the center of your life and wonder what the meaning of all of it is. The answer is not abstract. The answer is you. You are what it means to be here. The how of that truth is what we are working toward. But modern life pushes us forward constantly. Faster. Harder. "Go," it says. "Achieve. Improve. Produce. Don't stop." So you don't.

You run on a treadmill, proud of the miles you think you've gained, never questioning whether the ground beneath you has moved at all. Know that it is okay to stop while the world rushes past and ask: *What am I running toward? Who told me I had to get there?*

With one foot before birth and one foot after death, we find that we stand, in truth, with our feet together. Time collapses. Urgency collapses. And the illusions we've lived inside begin to crack. The house of mirrors shatters, revealing itself for what it is. This is maya lifting—not all at once, but the way fog burns off when the sun rises.

Burn out or radiate?

Stress or softness?

Overwhelm or overcome?

These are not spiritual binaries. They are choices. Meditation creates the space where those choices live. It teaches you to place awareness between you and the world, between stimulus and response, between expectation and obligation. Once you feel that space, you see clearly: some of what affects you is yours, and much of it is not. You begin to sense what belongs inside your mind and what never should have entered.

As I promised earlier, unwelcome thoughts and unwelcome moments will always exist. That's simply consciousness doing what consciousness does. But once you learn to create space—the same space you created in your body scan, now in your life—you begin to choose your battles instead of being conscripted into all of them.

This moment appears in many traditions. You don't need to have read the *Bhagavad Gita*, but one piece from it fits perfectly here. On the battlefield, Arjuna collapses, not from fear of death but from fear of acting without understanding. He sees the world pushing him into a role he didn't choose. Krishna does not tell him what to do; he teaches him how to see. Only then can Arjuna choose his action with clarity.

You face that same moment in modern form. Different field, same fear. And it leads to a question that quietly begins shaping a meditative life: *To whom do I allow to interrupt my peace?* This is a declaration of agency.

The practicality of meditation becomes obvious once you feel this shift. It gives you clarity to see what you've attached yourself to, what's been driving you, and where you've been living on autopilot. If you've felt like you were drowning under stress or anxiety, this is the moment your head breaks the surface. You inhale differently. You operate from clarity rather than compulsion.

Instead of reacting blindly just to survive your life, you begin noticing it before you respond. You see the moving parts. You see the triggers before they trigger. You see the systems you obeyed because you didn't realize disobedience was possible.

Meditation hands you the reins you never realized you'd dropped. It doesn't give you a new destiny or a new identity. It gives you the space to steer the one you already have. Clarity is the doorway. Agency is the walk through it. And what you build from here becomes the true practical application.

2

Before going any further, it's important to recognize that even the simplest tools you've learned so far—a body scan, a steadied breath, and the ability to observe a thought—already give you more influence over your inner life than most people ever discover they have.

Most emotional spirals begin in the body, not the mind.

A tightened jaw becomes worry.

A shallow breath becomes dread.

A clenched abdomen becomes a catastrophic narrative.

Once you start noticing these sensations before the storyline forms, the entire spiral loses momentum. A few moments of awareness can interrupt hours of unnecessary psychological fallout, and this happens not through force but through recognition. Automaticity dissolves when it is seen clearly.

Breath offers another point of influence. When you lengthen the exhale, you change the physiological environment in which your mind is operating. This isn't metaphor; it's neurology. Dr. Stephen Porges explains: "When feeling stressed or overwhelmed, use breath as an anchor and focus on it. Slowing down exhalation promotes the dominance of the parasympathetic system, which can help you bring your body back to a calm state of safety."

A longer exhale doesn't produce calm. It creates the biological conditions that make calm possible. It shifts the nervous system out of its reactive mode so the mind can interpret the world from a grounded state rather than a defensive one. Short exhales keep the system on alert; long exhales disrupt the pattern. The mind follows the body's lead because it must.

As for thought, beginning to hear the tone, cadence, and architecture of your inner monologue marks a significant shift. Most people obey their thoughts reflexively, mistaking familiarity for truth. But when you observe thought without immediately enacting it, you begin recognizing the difference between content and command. This alone changes the internal architecture of choice.

From these basic skills emerges something surprisingly new: the sense that you have room to respond. Not dramatic choices, but subtle ones—the inflection of your voice, the interpretation of an email, the decision to wait three seconds before speaking. Over time, these micro-choices accumulate into a shift in how you move through your own mind.

The body scan reveals another truth: how much tension you've been carrying without noticing it. Most people live in a baseline of physical bracing they never agreed to. Awareness doesn't dissolve tension instantly, but it exposes it. And once exposed, tension begins to lose its authority.

These basic tools also give rise to moments of presence— the brief, unforced intervals where breath is simply breath, body is body, and thought hasn't yet assembled a storyline. Not enlightenment. Not transcendence. Just moments where the mind stops adding commentary long enough for you to actually inhabit your life. Ephemeral moments of aum will begin to accumulate in frequency and duration. And it is all seeded in the basics.

3

None of this requires longer sessions or elaborate routines. I care not for the breadth of time but for the depth of my tea— meaning, the quality of attention matters far more than the length of the sit. Ten distracted minutes will never do what sixty honest seconds can. Depth has never been measured in duration. It is measured in how fully you are willing to inhabit the moment you're in.

What deepens the practice is not the addition of new techniques but the refinement of sensitivity. Returning to the same basic exercises—body, breath, thought—reveals layers that were invisible before. A body scan shows small muscles holding tension you never acknowledged. A breath becomes a diagnostic instrument for the emotional weather system unfolding within. A thought displays its tone and origin instead of masquerading as truth.

This refinement appears because you stayed. You stayed long enough to notice what you once outran. You stayed long enough to tell the difference between discomfort asking to be softened and discomfort asking to be understood. Deepening is not endurance; it is the simple decision not to abandon yourself at the first sign of internal friction.

Consider a familiar moment: you're in the kitchen at the end of a long day. A bowl slips from your hand and clatters across the floor; sauce splatters everywhere. Usually, this would ignite a flare of irritation. But before the irritation forms, you feel the breath shorten and the shoulders rise. Because you notice this, the irritation never becomes anything larger. The mess didn't matter. The event didn't matter. Everything is always happening. What mattered was the reaction that never had the chance to take control.

Another moment: you receive that kind of text from that person. The trigger hasn't changed, but the experience has. You notice the tension appearing, almost like a habit trying to stand up. The text is only a thing brought to you. Your reaction is the thing that once made it feel like an attack. Seeing the pattern early changes everything.

These moments are the real deepening. Not the hours sitting cross-legged, not the ornate techniques people adopt when they want to feel spiritual. Depth is built in small corrections to ordinary moments. It is built in waiting at a red light, in the silence of an elevator, during the two seconds before the next task begins. These unremarkable fragments of a day are where the mind is most transparent, most unguarded, most workable.

Complex practices will come later, but they will not replace these fundamentals. They rely on them. Without this sensitivity, advanced techniques become performance. With it, even a single breath is sharp enough to cut through years of habitual reactivity.

Staying is what deepens the practice. Staying with the breath long enough to see what it's doing. Staying with the body long enough to hear what it's holding. Staying with a thought long enough to understand its origin instead of its volume. Depth grows not because you try harder, but because you stop leaving so quickly. Presence, once available in small pockets, expands on its own.

4

All that ever happens is everything. Life doesn't pause so you can process one thing at a time. It moves as a single, continuous field—one moment rising while another falls. The ocean doesn't work in shifts; the waves do not stop so the next wave can take its turn. Experience works the same way.

What matters is not the stream of events but the moment you notice yourself forming a reaction inside them. Epictetus said, "We are not disturbed by things, but by the view we take of them." He wasn't offering comfort. He was describing the mechanics. The event is external. The reaction is internal. The life you feel is the combination of both.

When you begin observing the reaction instead of collapsing into it, something uncommon happens: the mind hesitates. Not from confusion, but from clarity. In that brief hesitation, you encounter aum—not as a sound or mantra, but as a moment of unburdened awareness before interpretation begins. Aum is the instant before the mind decides what the moment means. It is the clean space in which you recognize the possibility of choice.

Whether you act or stay still, whether you turn toward or away, begins in that aperture. Aum doesn't choose for you any more than the supermarket fills your basket. It reveals that a choice exists. Without awareness, everything pushes you. With awareness, everything becomes something you can meet.

We do not control what arises.

We control how early we notice our part in it.

5

What you've built in this chapter is orientation. You now know where the hinge of your experience sits. You know where reactions begin. You know what tension feels like when it forms, not just when it overwhelms. Hopefully an image of a fulcrum begins to emerge.

This is enough for now.

Before adding depth or duration, let these recognitions settle. Meditation is not a curriculum. It is a shift in how you meet your life. These openings, small as they are, will begin to show up on their own.

The next chapter will not complicate the practice. It will integrate it. It will show how awareness begins to move with you through a day without being forced.

For now, it is enough to know this:

you have already begun.

The Ocean and All Its Devices

In the dim, I turn —

not the body, but the depth

I forgot I held.

1

You have already begun. The doorway has opened, the hinge is visible, and the mind has slowed just enough for you to recognize that awareness appears before interpretation. But that recognition, as profound as it is, lives only in the mind. The next step is not mental. The next step is bodily. Awareness is not complete until the body responds. And what the body reveals is often older, deeper, and far less interested in your beliefs than your mind is.

The previous chapter ended in the moment before the next step. This chapter begins in the first step itself: when the mind loosens its grip and the body speaks for the first time in years.

That step arrived for me in a place I didn't expect: my first Reiki session.

I didn't go looking for insight. I didn't go hoping for transformation. If anything, I walked in indifferent, seeking only the experience of novelty. I have a rational mind, and rational minds aren't easily impressed by dim lights and soft music. I assumed I'd lie down for an hour, close my eyes, relax a little, and leave exactly as I arrived. This moment wasn't supposed to matter. It wasn't supposed to be a turning point. It wasn't supposed to be anything more than an appointment on a Tuesday.

The room was dim without feeling theatrical. A single lamp softened the edges of the space. A hint of sage lingered in the air, not in a way that announced spirituality but in a way that suggested someone had cleaned the air before I arrived. The music was ancient in tone but not exotic, something with a pulse older than its melody. The space didn't feel mystical or curated. It felt like a place where people go when they are tired. A place the body recognizes faster than the mind.

The Reiki Master asked me to lie down. The table was warm—not enough to feel indulgent, just enough to silence argument. Her hands began at my head. I felt a faint pulse beneath the surface, a small rushing of something moving—blood, breath, warmth. I dismissed it instantly. Probably tension releasing. Probably nothing.

Then her hand rested on my sternum, and the entire moment shifted.

It was immediate. My breath drew short and quickened. My pulse rose. And beneath her palm, something opened—something sealed, something old, something that had not been touched in a very long time. It felt like a chamber filling, the way water rushes into a room once a door finally breaks. It wasn't subtle. It wasn't symbolic. It wasn't poetic. It was unmistakably physical.

Warmth spread outward in slow, thick waves. It didn't feel seductive. It didn't feel emotional. It felt like blood returning to a place where blood should have been all along. A fullness rose in my chest's hollow, as if the body had been waiting for permission to breathe fully.

Then came the movement. A slow, internal rotation, not muscular but deep and circular, like an interior wheel turning once and then again. The sensation didn't feel imagined. It didn't feel metaphorical. It felt ancient. Organic. Mechanical in the way that evolution is mechanical. An ouroboros stirring in the dark. My senses were telling me that I was continually rotating, although my body was firmly set on the bed.

This wasn't intimacy in the sexual sense. It was intimacy in the primal sense—the kind of intimacy that occurs when the body finally stops lying about how much it has been holding. Intimacy, which comes from *intimus*: innermost, deepest, to make known, to impress. To be seen. To be connected. What more is there?

Her hand was steady, calm, permissive. The room felt safe in a way I did not define. The body defines safety differently than the mind. The mind needs explanation. The body needs permission. And in that moment, permission was given. It sounds paradoxical, the way in which being fully vulnerable can feel secure.

It felt like the room said:

lie down; this is where you come when you need to be made whole.

53

When the session ended, I didn't feel transcendent. I didn't feel transported. I felt calm. Deeply calm. Calm in a way that didn't require interpretation. Something inside me had unclenched, and it surprised me how little drama was attached to that release.

The part that stayed wasn't the intensity. It was the fact that none of it required belief. I walked in with skepticism, and my body responded anyway. It responded without consulting my preferences. It responded because something old inside me recognized the opportunity to open.

Only later did I understand what had actually happened. At the time, it felt like an anomaly. A strange physical event. But in truth, it was my first contact with the ocean beneath the surface. The depth that meditation prepares you to meet. The depth the mind rarely allows. The body didn't ask my permission. It simply opened. This chapter begins here because everything that follows—physiology, psychology, meditation, samsara—was contained in that single moment of surrender.

The body revealed what the mind had been holding shut. And it did so with a simplicity that felt more connected than anything I had read in any book or heard in any class. This is the body's language of waiting and holding. It opens when the mind stops interrupting.

2

At this shore of our own body, we fold back the lip of a wave, revealing the gentle gears and cogs that make us beautifully human.

What happened on that table felt mysterious only because I did not yet understand the machinery beneath the experience. The body is not subtle about the truth; it is only subtle when the mind refuses to listen. Once you know the biology, the entire moment becomes clear. What felt extraordinary was simply the body returning to its natural intelligence.

The first system to respond was the vagus nerve. If the nervous system were an ocean, the vagus nerve would be its tide. It determines whether the body moves toward vigilance or toward restoration. It influences heart rate, digestion, breath depth, emotional tone, and the feeling of "I am safe" or "I am under threat." When the vagus nerve activates, the entire internal world changes. Muscles soften. Breath slows. Blood vessels widen. The chest loosens. What people describe as peace, clarity, or "energy" is often nothing more mystical than this biological shift.

The sternum is a gateway to this shift. Beneath it lies the heart, lungs, and the childhood home of the thymus—an organ deeply tied to immune function and profoundly sensitive to stress. This region is the emotional front door of the body. People touch their chest instinctively during shock, grief, relief, or overwhelm. It's where the body stores the heaviness of unsaid things. When someone places a calm, steady hand over that area, the body recognizes the gesture immediately. It interprets it as stability, like a hand on the hull of a trembling boat.

Before the mind has time to form a story, the signal travels. The vagus nerve reads the pressure and warmth as a cue to release its grip. This is why the sensation hit me before I could think. The body moves faster than interpretation. It always has.

The warmth I felt spreading through my chest was vasodilation—the widening of blood vessels that occurs when the sympathetic (stress) system steps back and the parasympathetic (rest) system rises. Under stress, blood rushes to the core, preparing for action. Under safety, blood returns to the limbs, the skin, the surface. This is why fear chills and calm warms. That heat wasn't mystical. It was my circulatory system saying, finally.

The fullness beneath the sternum was the diaphragm releasing. Most people breathe like hunted animals: shallow, tight, vertical breaths. The diaphragm becomes rigid; the rib cage narrows; only the upper chest moves. When the vagus nerve activates, the diaphragm softens. Breath drops lower. The "fullness" is the body remembering how to breathe biologically instead of psychologically.

The circular movement—the strange, interior turning— belongs to the vestibular system. Under stress, the brain keeps a strict orientation: posture, balance, spatial awareness, micro-corrections. Under relaxation, it lets go. When vigilance drops, the inner orientation system recalibrates. People often feel this while falling asleep, during deep meditation, or after certain forms of touch therapy. It is not disorientation. It is reorganization. The ocean redistributing its weight when the wind calms.

Another layer: interoception. Interoception is the ability to feel the inside of the body without fear or interpretation. Chronic stress dulls it. The mind numbs sensation because feeling too much while you're trying to survive is dangerous. But when calm returns, interoception switches back on. Sensations once muted rise clearly. The heartbeat becomes audible. Breath becomes a presence. The sternum becomes a door instead of a wall. The interior becomes inhabitable.

This is why the experience felt intimate, not seductive. The body was letting me back in.

There's also somatic memory. The body stores emotional patterns in muscular and autonomic pathways long after the mind has forgotten the original causes. The sternum region in particular carries years' worth of bracing — tiny micro-contractions built from grief, anxiety, shame, unspoken emotions, disappointments, arguments, the constant vigilance of modern living. When that region softens, somatic memory stirs. This is not trauma release in the dramatic sense. It is the body relaxing out of habits it never meant to form.

Another system involved is predictive processing. The brain constantly generates predictions about what will happen next. It uses past experience to anticipate threats, tone, movement, danger, expectations. This predictive engine runs faster than consciousness. When her hand rested on my chest, and the environment remained consistently safe, the predictive engine stalled. There was nothing to solve. Nothing to analyze. Nothing to guard against. The mind briefly lost its habitual role as the narrator of the moment. That silence allowed the interior to rise.

Every physical sensation I felt — heat, fullness, rotation, softening — was the direct result of this pause in prediction. When there is no anticipation of threat, the body stops bracing. When bracing stops, the deeper systems activate. This is what people describe as "energy moving," "emotion releasing," "spirit opening," or "a wave rising." None of those descriptions are wrong. They're simply poetic interpretations of very old biological mechanisms.

And then there's co-regulation. Humans regulate their nervous systems through proximity to other calm nervous systems. A steady presence can shift another person's physiology without words. Infants regulate through caregivers; adults regulate through touch, voice, eye contact, and steady breath. Her calm presence—and her lack of agenda—allowed my system to entrain to hers. Co-regulation is not mystical. It is mammalian biology. It is why people calm each other down without speaking. It is why a warm hand over the sternum can undo years of tension.

Everything that happened was a precise sequence of biological shifts triggered by safety. The mind, for once, was not directing anything. The body was. And without the mind's interruption, the ocean beneath the surface rose into awareness. What felt profound was actually the absence of interference.

This is the physiology of surrender. Not surrender as defeat, but surrender as the release of unnecessary effort. The body knows how to descend into calm without being told. It knows how to let go of vigilance. It knows how to breathe deeply. It knows how to shift from survival to presence. It knows how to return to depth.

Meditation is the deliberate version of that process. It teaches the mind how to stop interrupting the body. It gives the body permission to do what it already knows how to do.

This is the bridge. Let's cross it.

3

Everything that unfolded during the Reiki session—the warmth, the opening, the quiet—felt powerful because it arrived without my intention. It felt like something happening to me, not something happening through me. But the truth is simpler and far more useful: meditation can recreate the same descent, not by accident, but by design.

Most people misunderstand meditation because they expect it to manufacture silence. They believe the goal is a mind without thoughts, a kind of interior blankness. But thoughts are the surface of the mind. Meditation is not an assault on thoughts. It is a slow turning inward toward what current runs beneath them. Everything that opened during that session opened because the mind stepped aside. Meditation teaches the mind how to do that intentionally.

Meditation begins with breath, not because breath is spiritual, but because it is one of few things both the conscious and unconscious mind can influence. The breath is the edge between the two. When the breath steadies—not forced, not manipulated, simply allowed—the mind begins to lose its habitual momentum. Thought becomes less sticky. Emotion becomes less urgent. The interior begins to appear.

Stillness comes next. When the body is still, the senses withdraw from the external world. Eyes closed, posture supported, no incoming demands. The world does not vanish, but the brain's need to interpret it fades. This is why meditation often feels like a dimming of interference. The mind no longer has a reason to stay braced. It begins to ease its grip.

Attention is the next movement. A drifting mind is not a problem; it is a default setting. The point of meditation is not to prevent drifting but to notice it early and return. Each return weakens the old habit of chasing rabbits. Each return strengthens a new habit of staying with what is actually happening. William James understood this when he wrote that the ability to bring back a wandering mind is the foundation of character. Meditation is that ability in practice.

A mantra—or any repeated sound or phrase—serves a simple function: it gives the mind a single, predictable point to rest on. Not to drown everything out, but to prevent the mind from generating more than is necessary. Repetition lowers cognitive noise. The mind stops rehearsing the next five minutes of life. It becomes a little quieter, a little steadier, a little more willing to release its need to narrate.

What meditation ultimately replicates from the Reiki session is not the sensation, but the sequence: the slow descent from surface to depth. The shift from doing to witnessing. The release of interpretation. The quiet that appears when the mind temporarily gives up its need to organize experience. The body opens on its own when the mind is not in the way.

This is why meditation feels familiar even the first time someone truly drops in. The body recognizes the descent long before the mind does. Meditation is not a foreign state. It is a returning to, rather than a going toward.

Meditation also replicates the intimacy of the session but in a different direction. In Reiki, the intimacy was the encounter between my body and another steady presence. In meditation, the intimacy is the encounter between awareness and self. Meditation makes the interior perceptible. It makes the mind's habits visible. It reveals the early stirrings of reaction. It shows the moment before a thought becomes a idea, before an emotion becomes identity, before the cogs begin to turn.

Aum emerges without announcing itself. Meditation strengthens that moment. It teaches the mind to recognize the earliest ripple. The breath steadies. The attention returns. The senses quiet. And in that small space between impulse and interpretation, moments of aum surface from within.

Meditation is the deliberate practice of accessing that moment again and again until the mind learns to pause before collapsing into its old patterns. The Reiki session opened the door for me accidentally. Meditation is the way a person learns to open it on purpose.

Everything that happened on that table was a descent into the body's depth. Meditation is how you learn to descend without needing the catalyst, the hand, the table, the room, or the external safety. What was offered to me in that session, meditation teaches a person to offer themselves.

4

From the practice to the architecture it works upon—from meditation to the configurations of the mind itself: the system ancient texts called samsara. The word has been surrounded by centuries of mysticism, but its essential meaning is not complicated. Samsara is the mind's momentum, the aimless wandering. It is the automatic looping of thought, emotion, memory, prediction, and habit. Not as philosophy, but as psychology. Not as karma across lifetimes, but as conditioning across moments.

Samsara is the wheel the mind runs when left unsupervised. It is the sequence that begins with a sensation, becomes a thought, becomes an interpretation, becomes a reaction, becomes identity, becomes bound law, becomes a story, and then repeats. The repetition is not intentional but inherited. Evolution built the mind to loop because looping was efficient. What kept our ancestors alive was not clarity but anticipation.

A rustle in the grass might have been the wind, or it might have been a predator. The nervous system learned to assume the worst, because the cost of being wrong in that direction was survival. The cost of assuming the best was death. Over thousands of generations, this bias shaped the architecture of the modern mind. Today, the rustle is an email, a tone in someone's voice, a memory, a deadline, the awkward silence— but the machinery reacts as though these incorporeal threats have very real, very close teeth. We calculate, ruminate, plan, and regret, all to our own self-predation.

This is samsara. The residue of evolutionary vigilance running inside a world that no longer requires it. We are not so far from the forests and the plains. We spent epochs without the luxury of comfort, stability, or anything resembling health insurance. We have not caught up. "The feelings that guide us were designed not for truth, but for reproductive success." — Robert Wright, *Why Buddhism Is True*

Samsara is also emotional patterning—old fears replaying themselves long after the original danger has passed. Anxieties repeating themselves not because they are true, but because they are familiar. A person's mind will replay the same worry because its function is designed to predict threats, not to evaluate whether the prediction is reasonable.

Most people never see these devices, because they are too busy being moved by them. They believe their thoughts are true because their thoughts arrive with urgency. They believe their emotions are accurate because their emotions arrive with force. They believe their habits are choices because their habits feel like preferences. When a fire alarm rings, you run out of the building. The wheel keeps on spinning, and because it doesn't cease, it feels like reality rather than momentum.

Joseph Campbell wrote, "The mind has to be challenged and dismantled; otherwise, it becomes a machine." He wasn't offering advice. He was describing something observable: the mind becomes mechanical when awareness dissolves. The machinery takes over. Reaction replaces perception. Habit replaces presence. Samsara is not a curse; it is an unconscious default.

Recognizing samsara does not require rejecting the self. It requires noticing how much of the self is automated. You can see this in the way irritation appears before you understand why, or the way anxiety rises before you locate its source, or the way a memory can command the emotional tone of an entire day. Life happens, and the reaction leaps forward without your consent. The wheel turns before you have a chance to step off.

Samsara is not just mental. It is embodied. The body reacts before the mind narrates. The stomach tightens before the story forms. The jaw braces before the memory is named. The shoulders rise before the fear becomes conscious. These micro-reactions accumulate, shaping posture, breath, tone, and behavior— slowly crumpling our lives. The machinery operates in the background, and people assume the background is simply who I am.

Meditation reveals that it isn't. Meditation slows the wheel enough to see the spokes. The same way the Reiki session revealed the body's depth when vigilance paused, meditation reveals the mind's machinery when attention stabilizes. You begin to notice the beginning of a thought instead of being swept into its middle. You recognize the early stirrings of

63

emotion before the narrative attaches. You sense the moment when a reaction is forming, not after it has already taken control.

This is why ancient texts described samsara as a cycle of suffering. Not because life is inherently painful, but because momentum obscures clarity. When the mind moves too quickly, everything feels personal. Every thought becomes truth. Every emotion becomes identity. Every habit becomes fate. Samsara is being pushed by your own conditioning without realizing you're being pushed.

The mind evolved to think before you think about thinking. To react before you reflect. To anticipate before you interpret. Samsara is simply the absence of awareness inside those sequences. It is automatic continuation without intervention.

Meditation begins to interrupt this, not by force, but by slowing. When the mind quiets, even slightly, something unusual appears: the ability to see the machinery while it's running. Not to stop it immediately, but to recognize that it is machinery. That distinction alone changes everything. Clarity does not dismantle samsara, but it breaks its illusion of inevitability.

When you begin to observe the wheel instead of spinning with it, you discover space. The same space that appeared as aum in the previous chapter. Meditation expands that space. It teaches the mind to rest inside the place of non-things, finding residence in the source from which the world arises.

The ocean metaphor returns here because samsara is the surface—restless, repetitive, wind-driven. The deeper waters of the mind are not turbulent; they are steady. Meditation does not calm the surface permanently. It teaches you to access the depth underneath. The surface can be chaotic. The depth remains untouched. Samsara is the surface. Awareness is the depth.

5

Once you understand samsara as momentum, meditation becomes something more precise: the deliberate interruption of that inertia. Not the destruction of it. Not the conquest of it. Just interruption. And interruption, when done consistently, rewires a life.

Most people imagine meditation as creating calm. Calm is only the side-effect. What meditation truly creates is friction — the slowing of automatic processes that normally run unchecked. It is this slowing that allows clarity to appear. Meditation is not the cultivation of a state; it is the weakening of the reflex to collapse into old states.

It interrupts emotional inertia. The mind loves to take the first flicker of feeling and expand it into a whole three act drama. A single discomfort becomes a mood, becomes a story, becomes an excuse. Meditation doesn't suppress emotion; it prevents its inflation. The moment you notice the beginning of an emotional swell, you catch it before it narrates itself into something larger than it needed to be.

It interrupts mental narrative-building when the mind wants to explain everything immediately. We simply must know why something happened, what it means, what it predicts for the future. Meditation teaches you to see that explanatory impulse before it takes over, the way you might see a match being struck before the flame spreads. You notice the start of the story before you become the character trapped inside it.

It interrupts anticipatory fear. So much suffering comes not from what is happening, but from what the mind thinks might happen next. Meditation teaches the mind to stay with what is real long enough for imagined threats to lose credibility. Anxiety is a prediction, not presence.

It interrupts identification with thought. Normally, a thought appears and the mind immediately says: That is me. That is my voice. That is my truth. Meditation creates the slightest separation between thought and identity. A thought becomes something you observe, not something you are. This becomes a liberating non-attachment point.

It interrupts reactive conditioning. Every person has patterns that fire automatically: defensiveness, withdrawal, people-pleasing, over-explaining, shutting down, escalating. These patterns activate before awareness. Meditation slows the reaction. It gives you a half-second of clarity to choose something new.

It interrupts the illusion of urgency. Meditation exposes how little in life actually requires immediate mental engagement. Most things can wait. Phones can be turned off and the world will keep turning. It becomes clearer just how many things are optional.

Most importantly, meditation interrupts samsara itself. It slows the wheel to see the spokes. It reveals how small the initial spark is that ignites the whole sequence of suffering. The mind does not need to be forced into quiet. It only needs to be slowed long enough for awareness to slip between the gears. Once awareness enters, the machinery doesn't stop but it does transfer power back to you.

People imagine transformation as a grand event. But transformation begins here, in the smallest interruption. The moment you notice the start of a reaction and do not immediately follow it, you are already free in a way you weren't the moment before.

This is why meditation feels like spaciousness. Spaciousness is not a euphoric state. It is the absence of being thrown around. It is the moment the wave no longer convinces the ocean that the ocean is the wave.

When a person sits long enough to feel the beginning of their own patterns, they discover something remarkable: the reaction does not have to complete itself. The wheel can stutter. The wave can fall without crashing.

6

People often think meditation is too abstract to help with ordinary life. They imagine it as something done by monks, or by people with too much time, or by those who prefer stillness to action. But meditation is not the opposite of living. It is the restoration of the ability to live without being pulled in every direction.

What makes meditation practical is not any single state it produces, but the skill it teaches that I keep stressing: the ability to notice the moment before the mind turns a drop of water into a storm. Meditation returns agency to the earliest part of experience, the part most people never see because they are already reacting by the time they notice anything at all.

When you meditate consistently, the body begins to reveal tension earlier. You feel the jaw tighten before the sentence forms. You feel the breath shorten before the worry arrives. You feel the shoulders rise before the defensiveness takes shape. With enough practice, these micro-signals no longer sneak past you. You become familiar with the way your body whispers before it shouts.

This familiarity of the physical feedback is practical because it prevents escalation. Suffering often begins not with a major event, but with a tiny unnoticed contraction. A narrowing. A moment you pushed away because you were too distracted to stay with it. Meditation teaches you how to stay with the smallest discomfort long enough to understand it before it becomes something larger and more dramatic.

Meditation also makes life more workable because it reduces confusion. Without meditation, emotion and thought arrive fused together, a single knot you spend all day trying to untangle. With meditation, the threads appear separately. You can feel the emotion without immediately needing to weave a story. Your mind is the loom and you choose what it is you wish to make or not make. This separation is clarity. And clarity is the most practical tool a person can have.

This practicality extends beyond the internal. When your interior is less chaotic, your relationships evolve. You stop projecting unfinished stories onto others. You hear what people say instead of taking authorship. You feel the tone of a room without being swallowed by it. You become someone who is not constantly interrupting their own presence. Meditation is practical because it restores the ability to meet life where it actually is, not where the mind imagines it to be.

The Reiki session showed me what the body feels like when the mind stops interrupting it. Meditation showed me how to stop interrupting it without needing someone else's hand on my chest. The physiology wasn't the miracle. The miracle was realizing the body knew what to do all along.

This groundedness is the beginning of integration. Meditation is not meant to stay on the cushion. It is meant to stand up with you. It is meant to walk into your day. It is meant to accompany you through conflict, conversation, intimacy, uncertainty, grief, joy. Meditation becomes a state you carry, not an activity you perform.

The inner, mental meditation is the moment before the next step. Moving meditation is the next step.

Yoga Flame

The moment stands still.

The body carries it forward.

Movement becomes breath.

1

Modern life shapes the human body in ways that our ancestors would not recognize. Hours spent driving, sitting at desks, reclining on soft furniture, and bending over small screens create postures that settle into the muscles like wet cement. Shoulders round forward, the upper back strains, the chest tightens, and the hips lose their natural capacity to open. The spine, which is designed to move like a supple branch, begins to behave more like a rigid beam.

Yoga offers one of the most accessible remedies for these accumulated patterns. Even if a person were to practice yoga solely for the physical benefits, without any spiritual or philosophical interest, the practice would still hold tremendous value. A body that moves through its full range of motion ages with greater ease. Muscles that engage regularly support the joints more effectively. Breath flows more freely through a frame that is not compressed by chronic tension.

There is an old saying that a person is only as old as the spine is flexible. Although the phrase sounds like folklore, it expresses something essential. The spine is not merely a column of bone; it is a living conduit for movement, sensation, and vitality. When the spine stiffens, the rest of life tends to stiffen with it. Movement becomes cautious. Daily tasks require more effort. A quiet fatigue settles in.

Yoga addresses this directly by inviting the practitioner to inhabit the full architecture of the body. The movements do not require athletic talent or aesthetic symmetry. They require attention to shape, breath, and alignment. Even simple poses, practiced consistently, awaken muscles that long ago surrendered to gravity and habit.

Many limitations turn out to be habitual rather than structural. The shoulders lift toward the ears because stress has taught them to live there. The hips resist opening because years of sitting have trained them into narrow confinement. The neck aches because it has learned to hinge forward toward screens rather than balancing naturally above the spine.

Through regular practice, these patterns begin to loosen. The body reclaims space that daily life has taken away. A person begins to notice lines of tension that were once invisible, emerging in the same way that stars appear when the sky darkens enough to reveal them.

Yoga adapts to bodies of every shape, age, and ability. Poses can be modified for injuries, limited mobility, or stiffness. The practice does not demand perfection; it encourages participation. A mat is optional. A studio is optional. What matters is the willingness to meet the body exactly as it is, without judgment or expectation.

This first step—waking the body and allowing it to move in ways it has forgotten—creates the foundation for everything that follows. Before yoga becomes a meditation, before it becomes a philosophy, it is an honest conversation with the physical self. Awareness will join soon, and breath will deepen, but the conversation begins here, in the muscles and joints that carry us through the world.

2

During any pose, the practitioner begins to notice small waves of discomfort or effort rising within the body. Muscles tremble. Balance wavers. Heat gathers. The mind reacts with habitual urgency, insisting on escape or collapse. Yet the breath offers a different instruction. It invites patience rather than panic. It reveals that the body can hold far more than the mind initially believes.

As the body shifts from one shape to another, a quiet juncture appears. It is a brief meeting point where awareness becomes precise, not because the posture is challenging, but because the transition exposes a delicate link between movements. In that link, the body performs a subtle articulation, reorganizing itself for what comes next. This small articulation often holds more clarity than the posture itself.

Awareness enters easily here, slipping into the movement at the exact moment the body prepares to change.

This is the beginning of moving meditation. Awareness rests not on a single object, as in traditional sitting practice, but on a continuous stream of physical sensation. The mind observes without interfering. The breath remains steady even as the body encounters strain, imbalance, or unfamiliar territory.

Yoga does not ask the practitioner to eliminate discomfort. It invites the practitioner to witness it without collapsing into it. Through this practice, a person begins to understand the difference between sensation and suffering, between effort and distress. The breath becomes a guide that leads awareness through the landscape of the body with clarity and steadiness.

Gradually, the body and mind begin to operate in unison, each supporting the other. Movement becomes the expression of awareness, and awareness becomes the quiet intelligence within each movement. The shape of the posture matters less than the quality of attention within it.

This union—breath guiding awareness, awareness guiding movement—is the foundation of yoga as a meditative practice. Everything that follows will grow from this point.

3

As the practice deepens, yoga reveals a quiet contradiction. The body is moving, yet the mind grows still. Muscles exert effort, yet a certain ease emerges within the effort itself. Strain arises, yet there is a softness inside the strain. The body meets limitation, yet awareness expands beyond it.

Each posture becomes a place where opposites meet without conflict. Breath steadies the mind even as the limbs tremble. Balance holds steady even as the body wavers. A calm interior remains available within moments of physical demand.

There is a point in the practice when the practitioner realizes that clarity arrives not after the effort, but within it. The paradox does not require resolution. It simply asks to be inhabited.

The pose holds you far more than you hold the pose.

This is the essence of moving meditation. In the middle of exertion, the mind discovers spaciousness. In the middle of motion, the mind discovers stillness. Awareness does not wait for comfort in order to appear; it appears precisely where comfort ends.

This is not an idea to analyze. It is an experience to notice. The paradox of yoga does not explain itself. It simply reveals itself, and then invites the practitioner to continue moving.

The purpose of learning to breathe and remain aware in uncomfortable postures is simple. The body does not reserve discomfort for the mat. It appears throughout daily life: the tightening in the lower back when standing from a chair, the heaviness in the legs after a long day, the sharp pulse of pain when a joint catches, the sluggishness of illness, the ache that arrives without warning, the stiffness that comes with age. Yoga trains the mind to remain steady inside these ordinary physical challenges. What begins as breath in a posture becomes breath in a moment of pain, breath in fatigue, breath in the movements that feel slower or more fragile than they once did. The body offers strain; the breath offers clarity.

A posture practiced with awareness becomes preparation for the times when the body falters. The steadiness learned during a long hold becomes steadiness when cold or illness saps energy. The breath maintained during imbalance becomes the breath maintained when vertigo, dizziness, or weakness interrupts daily activity. The patience cultivated in a challenging shape becomes patience in the middle of chronic discomfort or the slow ache that accompanies aging. The quiet space found within physical strain echoes the form of the quiet space needed when movement is limited, cautious, or painful. The mat becomes a rehearsal space for the days when the body feels heavy, unpredictable, or tender.

Discomfort on the mat reveals a truth that carries far beyond it: sensation is not the same as danger. Muscles trembling during a pose do not signal catastrophe any more than the sudden stiffness in the neck or a surge of joint pain signals collapse. Yoga teaches that physical discomfort does not demand panic. It demands attention, breath, and a willingness to remain present without tightening the entire body in anticipation. The breath becomes a stabilizing axis that keeps the nervous system from spiraling into fear-based reactions.

This training prepares a person for the countless physical interruptions that shape a life. Waking up stiff, navigating a flare-up of inflammation, dealing with chronic pain that ebbs and flows, feeling the body heal unevenly after an injury, or simply moving through a day when the body feels heavier than the mind wishes it were—these are opportunities to apply what the practice taught. Awareness meets the sensation calmly. Breath slips between the body's protest and the mind's interpretation. Movement becomes slower but clearer. Even on days when mobility is limited, the relationship between breath and awareness remains intact.

Over time, something shifts. The practitioner no longer braces against pain with the entire body. The breath arrives first. The awareness settles second. The physical reaction follows last, softened and deliberate. This sequence becomes a reflex shaped by repeated experience on the mat. Yoga does not remove discomfort; it reorganizes the way the body and mind respond to it. The body becomes not an adversary but a companion, speaking in sensations that no longer feel overwhelming.

This is why yoga is more than movement. It is preparation for the realities of living in a body that will experience fatigue, injury, illness, aging, limitation, and vulnerability. It is how meditation stands up, enters the day, and remains present when the body begins to struggle. The clarity cultivated on the mat becomes clarity in the mornings when movement is slow, in the evenings when pain is sharp, and in all the moments when the body demands patience rather than resistance.

4

Yoga does not require youth, strength, or flexibility. It requires willingness. A person can begin at any age, in any condition, and with any range of ability. The body may feel unsteady, tight, or unfamiliar at first, but this is not a barrier to the practice; it is the beginning of it. Every posture can be adapted. Every movement can be slowed. Every breath can be met exactly as it is.

For those who have never stepped onto a mat, a simple beginner routine is more than enough. A short video in the living room will teach as much about the body as any formal class. A sturdy chair, a wall, or even the edge of a bed can support the movements when balance feels uncertain. The goal is not beauty or precision. The goal is attention. When the breath remains steady, even a small motion becomes an entire practice.

If practicing at home feels supportive and a person wishes to go further, a skilled instructor can be a valuable guide. A knowledgeable teacher can help remove early stumbling blocks, protect the joints through proper alignment, and adapt movements for injuries or limitations. Yet instruction is never a requirement. Many people deepen their practice entirely through simple routines at home. A class is an option, not a necessity, and it is important that no one feels excluded by cost, scheduling, or circumstance. Yoga begins wherever the body is, and it remains fully available whether practiced alone or with guidance.

Progress arrives quietly. The body begins to release tension that once felt permanent. Movements that were difficult become possible. Pain that once demanded bracing becomes something the breath can accompany with steadiness. None of this happens quickly, and none of it needs to. Yoga unfolds through repetition, not intensity.

If the body resists certain shapes, that resistance is not failure. It is simply information. The practice meets the body as it is, not as it once was or as someone hopes it might be. There is dignity in beginning with what is available. There is wisdom in allowing the body to lead rather than forcing it into ideals.

Yoga is not something reserved for quiet rooms or perfect conditions. It can slip into moments throughout the day: stretching gently upon waking, breathing deeply while standing at a sink, shifting posture during long hours of sitting, pausing before rising from a chair. Each of these is part of the practice. The body offers endless opportunities to return to awareness.

Yoga is one expression of moving meditation, but not the only one. Any practice that unites breath, awareness, and physical motion carries the same possibility for clarity, whether the movement is large, small, slow, or barely perceptible.

The invitation is simple: begin where you are. Move the body with patience. Breathe through the movements with attention. Notice the details that daily life teaches you to ignore. In time, clarity emerges not only from stillness but from motion. The body becomes both the path and the companion.

Yoga is not a destination. It is a way of shaping presence inside the limits and possibilities of the human frame. Even the smallest effort carries a person forward. The practice does not ask for perfection. It asks for sincerity. And sincerity is always enough.

The Body Listens First

Bowls shimmer like rain.

Inside their trembling chambers,

the quiet finds you.

1

There is another layer to the meditative practice: sound, which can both fill the volume of space and soothe the mind to a quiet. The formal setting for this is the sound bath. And Kate Gajewski, proprietress of *Be the Lightness, Inc.*, is a master guide of auditory journeys.

I met with Kate in her studio, where she gave thoughtful insight into the work she does and how it becomes a practical tool for the meditative mind. What became clear immediately is that sound, for her, is not performance. It's not even technique, although the technique is there. It's listening. It's presence. It's responding to the nervous system the way someone might soothe a crying child or a startled animal—without words, without strategy, simply with attunement.

She works with an array of instruments: bowls, gongs, chimes, shells—tones that rise like breath and fall like rain. She knows which sounds tend to anchor people and which tend to lift them, but she doesn't arrive with a set plan. "I don't have a framework before I come in," she told me. "It just flows intuitively."

It struck me how closely this mirrors internal meditative work. Once you understand the territory, effort becomes interference. The body knows what it needs—if the mind will just get out of the way long enough for the body to speak. Sound does that for people. It removes the part of practice that feels like practice.

She said something else that rang true to my own experience: "With sound, you don't have to do anything. There's nothing to think about or focus on. You just receive."

This mirrors what was discussed in the Reiki chapter: the body already knows how to downshift into parasympathetic states, but the mind often won't allow it. Sound bypasses that mental gatekeeping. It offers sensation instead of instruction, vibration instead of analysis.

Once vibration enters the body, physiology takes over.

The bowls, the gong, the tones—they do not activate imagination the way words do. They activate breath. They activate fascia. They stimulate the vagus nerve in ways that echo gentle touch. The parasympathetic system doesn't require a lesson to activate. It needs relaxation, immersion, and safety. Sound delivers that by design.

Through her lens, Kate—the sound-maker—is also an active listener. She said she watches very little. What she does is listen: breath, rhythm, small movements.

"I can gauge where they're at by their breath," she said.

It fascinates me that while the minds of twenty people may be going twenty different directions, breath is a far more honest report of where the nervous system actually is. Some drop quickly. Others fight it. Others hover, dipping down and rising back up. But when the room collectively deepens—when breathing slows and lengthens—she knows everyone has crossed a threshold.

"By the time I'm playing the gong," she said, "everyone is somewhere else."

Somewhere else: not another dimension, not another plane, but a quieter layer of their own system. A place beneath thought, beneath vigilance, beneath the need to manage themselves.

It reminded me of aum: the vibration that precedes articulation. Aum is not a syllable; it's the sensation of slipping under thought into the raw hum of existence. Sound baths recreate that access point externally. The vibration comes from outside you but opens into something inside you.

She demonstrated how the instruments themselves inform her choices. Some bowls seem to "belong" near the chest. Some tones meet the lower body. Some open the head space. Some rumble through the rib cage and loosen grief. She wasn't presenting doctrine—just years of noticing what people report afterward.

She said certain bowls "support letting go," especially those aligned with transformation or release. She wasn't being

81

mystical—just practical. Different frequencies inhabit the body in different ways.

What matters is that these sounds don't encourage prediction.

They don't create rhythm the mind can chase.

They don't invite narrative.

They unfold.

And when the mind stops predicting, the rest of you can finally participate.

The instruments used in a sound bath are not played in melodies or patterns. There is no cue for the mind to anticipate what is coming next. The sounds are undefined: a music that encourages stillness, not dance. "When you cannot predict what will come," she revealed, "the mind stops trying to figure out what's coming next and it surrenders."

This links directly back to Reiki: the moment the mind stops gripping, the vagus nerve relaxes, the diaphragm softens, heart-rate variability improves, and the system begins to repair itself. Sound simply gets people there through vibration instead of hands-on work.

Kate told of her first sound bath—how there were only two instruments and how she had underestimated them. But then the gong began, and everything dropped away. "It was the most powerful experience I ever experienced," she said. "It was the first time I ever cleared my mind."

She sat in her car for an hour afterward, unwilling to disturb the state she was in. I understood that completely. When sound reorganizes you, the world outside feels too sharp to return to right away.

She found a trainer a week later. "I bought that gong," she said, laughing, "and I had no idea how I was going to get to play it for people, but I knew I would." There's something deeply human about a life pivot that begins not with a plan but with recognition.

While finding a local studio is best; if that is not accessible to you, Kate suggests YouTube. Her recommendation is to always listen with headphones. She encourages beginners to buy a simple bowl—not to recreate a studio session, but because making vibrations with your own hands teaches the body to listen. And she reminded me that nature itself is a sound bath: rivers, wind, insects, trees—frequencies older than any instrument.

The larger point is that sound is not exclusive. It's not a luxury but a doorway. Sometimes the most accessible one.

"I highly recommend anyone to try it," she said, "especially if you feel intimidated by sitting meditation or breathwork. This for me was the gateway."

2

Most of us are afraid of silence because silence exposes whatever hasn't been processed yet. Sound gives silence a texture, a shape. It invites the mind to rest without demanding that it shut up. It's a form of being held, immersed, without force. Sound lets the body remember what rest feels like. And for many of us, rest is the most advanced practice of all.

Reiki introduces the idea that the nervous system can be influenced through subtle means. Sound shows that the nervous system can influence itself when given the right conditions. One modality works through touch; the other through vibration. Both access the parasympathetic state without asking the conscious mind for permission. They each just do it in their own language.

3

A sound bath is not something you perform. It is something you enter. And once you're inside it, you begin to understand that sound does its real work when you stop trying to manage the experience. People often arrive thinking they must "meditate harder," as if concentration were the mechanism. But sound does not require concentration. It requires willingness.

The session begins the moment you let the sounds come toward you instead of bracing for them. The bowls shimmer in widening arcs. The gong gathers itself, then releases a slow pressure through the room. You don't follow these movements. You let them reach you. The nervous system recognizes this more quickly than the mind ever will.

The unfamiliarity of the tones is intentional. They give the mind nothing to measure. No melody. No cadence. Nothing that satisfies the part of you that wants to predict what comes next. And once prediction loses its footing, breath changes. Muscles soften. The body begins to respond to the environment instead of the internal monologue.

Kate speaks about listening for these shifts rather than watching for them. Breath tells her everything she needs to know: the moment a person's exhale lengthens; the slight collapse of the shoulders; the quiet ripple that moves through a room when twenty people begin to settle at the same time. Some drift quickly. Others hover at the edges. Others move in and out like a tide. But there is always a moment when a collective settling occurs, and she knows the room has crossed its threshold.

When the gong enters, the experience deepens. Its resonance travels differently. It doesn't feel played so much as released into the space. It moves through the body the way wind moves through the forest—subtle, steady, impossible to locate at its source. There is a quality to it that recalls a line I've always kept close from Samuel Taylor Coleridge: "Where Alph, the sacred river, ran / Through caverns measureless to man." A movement through unseen chambers. A sense of depth without map or boundary. Something widening beneath thought.

You meet this kind of sound by allowing it to carry you the way a leaf yields to a quiet lake. The leaf doesn't create its own movement; it receives what the water is already doing. The ripples come from below, spreading inward before they spread outward, reorganizing the surface long before you notice the change. Sound works the same way: it rearranges the inner space without requiring you to shape it. Vibrations have a way of doing and undoing things.

The practice is not transcendence. It is coherence. Not escape. Return.

Return to the rhythm beneath your thoughts, the one the body recognizes immediately when permitted the space. Sound closes the distance between awareness and physiology until they're no longer working against each other. It softens the system, steadies the breath, clears the static.

4

Meditation is not silence or sound. It is not stillness or movement. Meditation, like the vibration of a gong, permeates all things. It is the resonance of a self letting go, permitting space where contentment can occupy. It is the gentle clearing that makes a path for whatever comes next. It is the quiet threshold where acceptance begins to breathe.

The Sweet Undoing

Two branches leaning

long before the wind arrives—

that is how want works.

1

It's strange how intimacy begins in places that never announce themselves. A sound bath fades, the last vibration dissolves into the ribs, and for a breath or two everything feels unreasonably clear. Then someone speaks beside you—nothing special, nothing profound—and the entire moment shifts. Not because of what they said, but because some quiet part of you leaned toward the sound without permission. This is where longing begins: in the attention, not the touch.

Desire has never needed fireworks. It works in micro-adjustments: the way your awareness narrows toward someone as if the room has been rearranged around them; the way your breath catches, not in panic but in recognition; the way some long-dormant interior warmth stirs as if waking up to the possibility of being met. Intimacy begins with these subtle openings. Before wanting someone's body, you want the way their existence changes yours.

We pretend we're afraid of rejection, but what unsettles us far more is the possibility of being seen accurately—recognized in a way we haven't curated. It's disarming when someone perceives you with the same clarity meditation has been trying to teach you. Suddenly your practiced calm feels porous. Suddenly your carefully contained life feels a little too exposed. Longing is not just wanting another person; it's the shock of wanting to be visible to them.

There's a kind of sweetness in that danger. A pull that feels both ancient and embarrassingly modern. You find yourself wanting to move closer, not because anything has been promised, but because something in you has already answered a question no one asked aloud. This is the earliest form of attachment—the quiet, unspoken hope that a moment might become a place to rest, even briefly.

Meditation teaches you to stay with sensation, but longing teaches you what sensation means. The mind tries to keep you safe with its neat categories, but the body is already opening, already listening, already betraying its preference. And the truth is this: you don't fall for a person; you fall for the version of yourself that wakes up in their presence. That's why desire feels dangerous. Not because it consumes you, but because it changes you just by arriving.

Aum often appears here—not as stillness, but as a soft widening inside the chest. A recognition that something sacred has entered the room wearing an ordinary face. You don't call it love. You don't even call it desire. You call it what it is: a moment where your world leans a few degrees toward someone else, and you realize, with a mix of hope and alarm, that you want the tilt to continue.

2

Longing doesn't arrive with fanfare. It begins as a slow pressure under the surface, the kind that redirects your whole attention before you consciously realize anything has shifted. It's not the sharp edge of lust but the deeper, heavier warmth that gathers in the center of your being and pulls everything in you toward one person with quiet inevitability. There is nothing mechanical about it. It feels ancient, as if some instinct older than thought has chosen a direction and the rest of you is simply following.

What unsettles people is not the desire to touch someone; it's the desire to merge with them in a way that feels almost mythic. You sense a soft widening inside yourself, a loosening of boundaries you normally guard without effort. Suddenly, the space you inhabit feels too small, too solitary, and their presence feels like an invitation to expand into someone else's atmosphere. Longing makes the interior world feel porous. You aren't just attracted — you are being moved.

This is where the early threads of attachment begin, long before any commitments or declarations. The body, in its old, uncomplicated wisdom, starts leaning toward the person who makes you feel more alive. Not with urgency or desperation, but with an unmistakable pull. It's the pull of wanting to be seen without arranging yourself. Wanting to be met without shrinking. Wanting to dissolve a little — not to disappear, but to be experienced more fully through another human being.

Tantric traditions have always understood that the ache is not a problem to fix but a guide. Western culture mistakes longing for neediness, but in truth, longing is directional. It points to where connection wants to unfold, where something inside you recognizes itself in another person and reaches for that recognition again. Meditation sharpens this awareness. You can sense when your attention lingers longer than it should, when silence between you thickens instead of fades, when even casual closeness feels charged in a way that rearranges the atmosphere.

The ache is the first bond. Before touch, before narrative, before anything outwardly visible, there is this internal gathering — this warm, steady pressure that says, without words, *I want to be met here. I want something inside me to answer something inside you.* You may not act on it. You may try to ignore it. But longing has already begun shaping the way you move through the moment.

What begins as a quiet pull becomes the foundation of everything that follows: desire, intimacy, attachment, and eventually the lessons of letting go. The ache is not the danger in intimacy. It is the doorway. And once you feel it, even faintly, you understand why people risk themselves for connection at all — because somewhere beneath the noise and caution, a part of you has recognized where it wants to belong, if only for a while.

3

There is a moment in intimacy that no meditation practice prepares you for. It doesn't arrive with touch, or even with desire. It arrives the instant your longing stops being abstract and becomes personal. Something in you starts reaching — quietly at first, then unmistakably. Not for pleasure. Not for novelty. But for contact so complete it feels like truth.

You feel it as a widening inside you, a ripple in the interior world you thought you had tamed. The breath changes. The room sharpens. You are suddenly, startlingly aware that you want this person not in theory but in fact. You want them close enough that their presence rearranges yours. It is not need, not yet, but the early shimmer of wanting to be met — deeply, honestly, without disguise.

And here is the part most people never admit: You want the deepest part of you to be met by the deepest part of them. Not filled, not claimed — just met, the way fire meets oxygen. A recognition, an answering, a joining without possession.

This is the pull beneath lust, the ache beneath longing. It is the instinct that makes two people orient toward each other without thinking. The body leans before the mind approves. The heart opens before the story is ready. Something in you begins moving toward them, even as another part tries to slow you down.

This is attachment in its infancy — not the sticky kind born from fear, but the molten kind born from desire that wants to be witnessed. You want your wanting to matter. You want your yearning to land somewhere soft. You want the fire inside you to have a place to burn that isn't only your own skin.

This isn't desperation. This is the human condition at its most luminous. Longing is not a flaw; it is the bridge that makes connection possible. Without longing, intimacy has no direction. Without ache, desire has no depth. Without this early pull of "come closer," nothing in the world of touch ever becomes meaningful.

And yet, even here, something quieter moves beneath the wanting: a faint awareness that this pull—beautiful as it is—can undo you if you grip it too tightly.

That realization is what will carry us toward the next turn of the chapter. Because longing, left unchecked, becomes clinging. And clinging is where suffering begins. But longing itself? Longing is holy. Longing is heat that doesn't yet burn. Longing is the body saying, "Here is where I want to open."

And opening is how intimacy begins.

4

Longing is generous at first. It asks nothing. It only stirs. But sooner or later, the wanting grows teeth—not sharp ones, just enough to remind you that connection, real connection, is never neutral. Desire becomes risk the moment you realize you could be changed by this person.

It's subtle. Not dramatic. Not cinematic. Just the quiet recognition that if they leaned in—even slightly—you would meet them without hesitation. And that scares us far more than rejection ever could. Rejection wounds the ego; being moved threatens the entire architecture of who we think we are.

You feel it in the shift beneath your breath—not a tightening, but a kind of readiness. The heart doesn't beat faster; it beats truer. Your awareness sharpens the way it does when you're standing near the edge of something beautiful and dangerous at once. Not because you might fall, but because you want to.

This is the slippery threshold where people start to confuse longing with fate, intensity with intimacy, presence with possession. The mind rushes in, wanting labels, guarantees, a blueprint for what comes next. But desire doesn't offer blueprints. It offers openings. It offers the possibility of being met. And possibility is always a gamble.

Here's the uncomfortable truth: wanting someone deeply means accepting that you cannot stay the same if they walk toward you. This is the real risk—not heartbreak, not rejection, not the uncertainty of where things might lead. The risk is transformation.

Because when two people get close enough, they stop interacting with each other's surfaces. They start disturbing each other's depths. They awaken parts of themselves they forgot were alive. They light up rooms inside the psyche that had gone dusty from disuse. They stir hunger, softness, fear, hope—all in one bewildering sweep.

This is why desire feels sacred and destabilizing at the same time. You're not just drawn to their body or their energy—you're drawn to the version of yourself that appears in their presence. The way you soften. The way you listen. The way you become more permeable to the world.

But every sacred longing has a shadow.

The shadow is the impulse to hold, to secure, to make certain a moment that was never built for certainty. It's the instinct to bind what is still blooming. To guarantee what cannot be guaranteed. And this is where the chapter begins bending toward non-attachment—not by moralizing desire, but by revealing the point where desire becomes fear in disguise.

For now, stay with the ache. Stay with the wanting that feels like possibility, not prison. Because the moment the longing becomes a demand, the moment wanting becomes clinging, the moment heat becomes hunger to possess—that is where suffering enters the room.

5

Longing begins as something spacious. It opens you, widens your interior, brings color back to places that had gone dull. It feels like expansion—like the body has suddenly remembered it was built for warmth and connection. But longing has a second phase, one quieter and far more intimate. It begins when desire stops being a feeling and starts becoming a story. A story about what this person could mean, who you might become with them, or who you fear you won't be without them. This is the moment where wanting starts to curl into holding.

It doesn't happen dramatically. There's no clear boundary, nothing you can point to as the beginning of attachment. It's simply a subtle internal shift from "let me feel this" to "let me keep this." The desire that once opened you now tries, gently and instinctively, to secure its source. Attachment enters softly, as a tightening around a hope—the hope that the person will stay, that this atmosphere will continue, that what you're feeling is shared. You're not asking for guarantees, yet part of you is already behaving as if one has been offered.

This is where longing starts to grow roots. You notice yourself orienting around them in small, almost invisible ways. You replay details. You anticipate their replies. You imagine the next moment before this one has finished happening. The longing that once felt like freedom now has direction, gravity, momentum. Not unhealthy. Not needy. Just unmistakably charged with meaning.

This is also the point where suffering becomes possible — not because the desire is wrong, but because imagination begins to outrun reality. Attachment begins the moment the mind starts negotiating with longing: defining it, protecting it, insisting on it. You start scanning the space between messages. You read tone into their pauses. You feel the faint anxiety of wanting something to continue without knowing if it will. The body does not struggle here; the body simply wants to be met. It is the mind that claws at the future, trying to secure what touched it so deeply.

This shift is not a flaw. It's human. It's the natural consequence of being moved by another person. But it is also the moment where confusion can easily take root — when you might mistake the ache for fate, the pull for promise, the vulnerability for loss. If you don't recognize the transition, longing becomes defensive. It stops being a current and starts becoming a claim.

This section lives right on that edge — the place where desire begins to feel like investment, and where the mind starts gripping before you realize the hand has closed. What matters now is learning to notice it, to stay awake inside it, because this is where the teaching of non-attachment quietly begins: wanting fully without collapsing into possession.

6

There is a moment in every unfolding connection when
wanting stops feeling like a breeze and starts feeling like
weather—something with weight, direction, and the power to
rearrange you. It happens quietly, almost innocently. You don't
announce it to yourself. You simply notice that your attention
has begun to orbit someone rather than merely drift toward
them. Longing, once expansive, begins to narrow its focus. It
becomes personal.

This is where the emotional stakes increase. Wanting
someone feels beautiful; needing them to want you back feels
precarious. The shift is almost imperceptible: the difference
between enjoying a moment and depending on it, between
savoring closeness and fearing its absence. You catch yourself
hoping they'll text first. You imagine what their silence means.
You start interpreting their timing, their tone, their hesitations.
You're no longer meeting the moment; you're tracking it,
guarding it, trying to read its future.

Nothing about this is shameful—attachment biology is
older than language. But it complicates the emotional
landscape. The mind begins to weave small futures, tiny
predictions, soft assumptions. You start building a version of
them inside you, a version shaped less by who they are and
more by what you hope they might be. The tenderness that
originally opened you now begins to brace. The desire that
once flowed freely now gathers itself into something tighter,
more cautious, more afraid of being misunderstood.

This is where vulnerability reveals its teeth. Because now, if
they turn away—even slightly, even accidentally—it lands
inside you as disproportional meaning. Not because you're

irrational, but because the body reads withdrawal long before the mind can contextualize it. A slower reply. A distracted tone. A small change in their attention. Biological systems interpret these tiny shifts as destabilizing, even when nothing catastrophic is happening. You're invested enough to feel the wind change.

Wanting them is still beautiful here, but beauty blends with ache. You don't just desire them anymore—you desire continuity. You want them to respond, to reciprocate, to stay attuned. You want to feel chosen, not just enjoyed. And none of that is wrong. It's the architecture of connection. But this is also the exact terrain where the suffering begins, because the more tightly the desire coils, the less freedom the moment has to breathe.

This is where the emotional friction of intimacy becomes unavoidable: you are no longer just opening. You are beginning to cling. Not with desperation—just with human hope. But every hope has an underside, and that underside is the fear of not being met. The mind starts trying to secure what touched the heart. It starts negotiating, interpreting, protecting. The innocence of desire evolves into the caution of attachment.

This is the hinge. This is where all spiritual teachings on longing and love enter the room—not to stop desire, but to soften the grip forming around it. Because if longing is the spark, holding is the flame, and clinging is the burn. And unless you learn the difference, you will confuse the burn for the warmth you came seeking.

7

There comes a point in every deepening desire when the longing stops being something you feel and starts becoming something you are. The shift is subtle but unmistakable. You begin to measure yourself—your day, your mood, your sense of worth—by the temperature of their attention. A message from them lifts you. Silence from them pulls at you. Their presence rearranges your interior weather in a way you can't quite hide from yourself.

This is where the self begins to blur at the edges.

Not because you've lost yourself—nothing dramatic is happening externally. But internally, your emotional center starts migrating. You check your phone not out of habit, but out of hope. You replay moments not to analyze them, but to feel connected again. You construct small futures without meaning to. A version of you is forming that orients toward them without conscious permission.

This is the part of intimacy few people admit: desire wants union, but attachment wants definition. You don't just want them anymore—you want to know where you stand. You want to feel chosen in a way that proves the opening wasn't yours alone. You want confirmation that what's moving in you is moving in them.

And underneath all of that is the deeper truth: You've begun to imagine yourself with them.

Not in the grand cinematic sense—no weddings, no mortgages—just woven into the fabric of your ordinary days. You picture the sound of their voice in your kitchen. You imagine their laugh in the car beside you. You think of how their presence might alter the shape of your evenings. It isn't fantasy; it's orientation. Your inner world has started reorganizing itself around the possibility of them.

Attachment is born exactly here.

Not in passion, not in sex, not in confession; but in the quiet, internal moment when your identity begins to lean. This leaning is soft but its implications are enormous. Because once they occupy emotional space inside you, everything they do becomes meaningful. Their attention feels like sunligtht. Their distraction feels like shade. You feel warmed or chilled by things they don't even realize they're doing. It's intoxicating, yes. But it's also dangerous in a way intimacy always is: you've begun to outsource a small part of your emotional equilibrium. This is how humans bond. This is how humans break. The same mechanism does both.

And this is why the spiritual traditions speak so carefully about desire—not to kill it, but to understand the transformation it initiates. Because desire begins in the body, but attachment settles in the self.

8

All of this: the ache that knows your name, the hunger that starts to speak, the slow migration of your center toward another person—gathers into a single, uncomfortable truth: intimacy doesn't just stir feeling. It rearranges who you are inside your own life. At first it's expansion, color flooding back into places that had gone gray. Then, almost without warning, the expansion starts to curl inward. The wanting that once felt like a gift starts to feel like something you could lose.

Desire opens you. Attachment begins the moment you decide you cannot bear for that opening to close. That decision is rarely conscious. It shows up in smaller ways: the way your day brightens or dims depending on a reply, the way your attention hovers around their absence, the way your mood starts to track the rise and fall of their availability. You're not being dramatic; you're being human. The system that evolved to bond with caretakers now bonds with lovers, and it does not care that you've read three books on boundaries. It cares that you have found a place where you feel more alive, and it wants that aliveness to stay.

This is where longing quietly shifts from encounter to insurance policy. You stop simply enjoying the warmth and start quietly asking it for proof. *Prove this is mutual. Prove this will last. Prove I am safe here.* You may never say those words out loud, but your nervous system begins living as if the answers matter more than anything else. This is the point where intimacy, unchecked, can make your own life feel rented instead of lived—on loan from someone else's attention.

Meditation doesn't rescue you from this. It does something more honest: it lets you see it in real time. You notice the exact moment your hope tightens into demand. You feel when your chest no longer just opens, but braces. You hear the tone of your thoughts shift from let me meet this to let me keep this. That noticing is not cold detachment; it's clarity. It's the first time you can tell the difference between love and the fear of losing what love woke up.

Because here is the quiet dilemma at the heart of every deep attachment:

You want to give yourself fully and you want to remain yourself if it ends.

You want to lean all the way in and you don't want your center to live in someone else's pocket.

You want to be moved and you don't want to disappear.

Life doesn't ask you to choose between those. It asks a different question: *Who are you while you are wanting?* Not who you become when they adore you back, not who you become when they vanish, but who you are in the raw middle — while your whole system is reaching and you know how breakable that makes you.

To love with awareness is not to love less. It is to notice, with some honesty, where your peace has quietly become contingent on another person's behavior. It is to feel the pull, the ache, the fusion, and still remember there is a part of you that existed before they arrived and will exist after they leave. Not as a threat. As a fact.

The work that follows is not about closing the heart or cooling the body. It is about loosening the story that says, *If I lose this, I lose myself.* It is about finding the place in you that can hold longing without turning it into ownership, that can welcome closeness without turning it into a claim, that can say a full yes without secretly demanding a forever.

The Hand That Holds Too Tightly

I open my hand;

what was never mine to keep

rests lighter, then goes.

1

There is a quiet miser living inside each of us. Not the cartoon hoarder guarding coins in a dark room, but a subtler figure — the part of the mind that clings to anything it calls precious. We cling to people, moments, identities, pleasures, routines. The object doesn't matter. The grip does.

I noticed, at one point in my life, that everything I loved I held just a little too tightly. Not tight enough to crush, just tight enough that I thought I was keeping it close. But in that subtle tightening, I became the one held. I was trapped by the fear of losing what I cared about.

Clinging is not greed. Clinging is fear. Fear that if the thing leaves, I will not know who I am without it. A toddler shows us the truth in its purest form. Take their toy, their blanket, their crumb of a cracker, and the cry erupts immediately: *This is mine. I need it. If you take it, I will literally die!* Adults don't scream like toddlers. We simply suffer more quietly. The fear is the same.

Fear turns something simply loved into something desperately needed. It turns the open hand into a fist. And nothing can breathe inside a fist.

But the heart works differently. What the heart wants, the heart gives. The heart does not hoard. The heart has no fear of running out.

There is a kind of wealth that has nothing to do with money. Wealth is not what we store, but what we can offer. True wealth is not abundance for the self, but abundance of the self — a fullness that naturally spills outward. A generous life comes from overflow, not accumulation. But overflow is impossible when everything is clutched.

Non-attachment doesn't ask us to stop loving, wanting, or enjoying the world. It simply asks us to loosen the grip — to recognize where love has hardened into clinging, where desire has turned into dependency, where something we cherish has quietly become the landlord of our peace.

The work is not to reject anything. It is to meet what we love with open hands.

2

Desire is not the problem. We are meant to want things. We are meant to enjoy the sweetness of being alive — warmth, touch, beauty, connection, novelty, the small pleasures that ripple through a day. Wanting is human. Wanting is natural.

Suffering begins only when desire hardens into something else. When the thing we enjoy becomes the thing we believe we must keep. That is the moment the open palm curls into a fist.

Clinging is the attempt to freeze reality in place. It is the belief that if we hold tightly enough, the world will stop changing long enough for us to feel safe. But nothing in nature has ever stayed still. Not for us, not for anyone.

You can feel the difference in your own body: enjoyment expands; clinging contracts. Desire breathes; attachment suffocates. The same sensation can be a celebration or a trap, depending on the way the hand shapes around it.

Some things can't survive being held at all.

Try to cradle a soap bubble and it bursts the moment your skin meets its surface.

What makes it beautiful is exactly what makes it impossible to keep.

Other things disappear the moment you reach for them.

A whisper offered in confidence is whole only when it floats freely.

Try to grasp it, trap it, repeat it, and it becomes silence again.

And the most essential things cannot be possessed without destroying yourself.

A breath is yours for a single moment.

Try to cling to it, and you suffocate.

Let it go, and you live.

This is what the mind does with everything it calls precious.

It tightens — not out of cruelty, but out of fear.

Fear turns something simply loved into something desperately needed. Fear convinces us that if we loosen our grip, we will lose not just the thing, but ourselves. And so we cling. We cling to people, to roles, to identities, to memories, to pleasures, to expectations, to routines.

We don't suffer because things change.

We suffer because we insist they shouldn't.

Clinging transforms desire into dependency.

Non-attachment transforms desire back into joy.

Desire moves through us effortlessly, like breath.

Fear tries to trap it, and in trapping it, we become the ones trapped.

The invitation here is simple:

notice where your hand tightens, and ask what it's afraid of.

That is where the work begins.

3

We build so much of ourselves out of temporary shapes.

A child playing with clay understands this without ever needing to say it.

The clay becomes a car, and then a horse, and then four little soldiers.

Each shape feels complete while it lasts.

Each one feels like it has a name, a purpose, a story.

But the clay never stops being clay.

That's how identity works, too.

We form ourselves from whatever is at hand — our name, our relationships, our routines, the things we keep in our pockets and the things we keep in our hearts. We gather these pieces around us and say, "This is me."

But underneath all of those shapes, something quieter remains.

Something that doesn't disappear when the shape changes.

The trouble isn't that we take a form.

The trouble is the moment we forget the form is allowed to change.

A life cannot stay fixed any more than clay can stay a car forever.

It was never meant to hold still long enough for us to worship it.

It moves, even when we pretend it doesn't.

And yet, there is something gentle in remembering this.

Something that softens the grip.

Something that lets us meet our own shifting with a little less resistance.

You don't need to abandon your shape.

Just don't mistake it for the whole of what you are.

Clay doesn't resist becoming a new form. It yields. It follows the hand. It allows itself to be reshaped by the moment. There is a kind of peace in that. And when we stop insisting that everything remain exactly as it is, a similar peace begins to form in us — quietly, naturally, without force.

4

There is a moment that stealthily comes, where wanting becomes holding and holding becomes fear. It happens faster than the mind can name, somewhere between the spark of desire and the quiet panic that whispers, *do not let this go.*

Most people never notice this moment. They leap from enjoyment straight into ownership, as if joy must be domesticated before it can be trusted. But between wanting and clinging is a subtle, essential space. And learning to feel that space is the beginning of non-attachment. It is the difference between having something and trying to keep it.

You know this difference in your own body. Enjoyment softens the shoulders. Clinging tightens the jaw. Joy widens the breath. Fear shrinks it. One expands you; the other protects you.

But protection against what?

Against loss.

Against change.

Against the devastating possibility that you might be asked to continue without the thing you love.

When we don't notice this shift, we confuse possession with safety. We think the world owes us continuity. We mistake proximity for permanence. We believe holding tighter will keep anything from leaving.

But you and I both know how this actually works: the tighter the grip, the less room anything has to breathe. Even tenderness suffocates when pressed too close.

The mind tells us, *If I loosen, it will slip away.*

But the heart answers, *If you loosen, you will finally feel it.*

Non-attachment lives in that tiny space where your hand relaxes, not in rejection, but in trust. Trust in yourself. Trust in life. Trust that what is meant to stay will stay, and what is meant to pass will pass without ruining you. You don't loosen to lose. You loosen to live.

When you pause in that space between holding and having, something remarkable appears: the thing you love becomes visible again. Not as an object to secure, but as a moment to experience. A person to meet. A feeling to savor before it naturally changes.

Nothing real is ever improved by clinging to it.

Nothing true requires gripping.

Nothing beautiful asks to be caged.

The open hand doesn't push away and it doesn't pull closer.

It simply meets what arrives as it arrives.

This is the quiet pivot that prepares the rest of the chapter: once you feel this space — even once — you understand what it means to enjoy without being owned, to love without losing yourself, to live without tightening.

This is where non-attachment stops being an idea
and becomes a way of touching the world.

5

Non-attachment is not an exit from life. It is a way of entering it more fully.

We should enjoy things. We are built to love deeply, laugh loudly, savor sweetness, and let ourselves be moved by whatever the day places in front of us. Pleasure was never the problem. Neither was beauty, or comfort, or closeness. The trouble begins when enjoyment becomes ownership. When the thing we like becomes the thing we fear losing. When a beautiful moment becomes a demand for repetition. When a relationship becomes a contract the world never signed.

Attachment tries to lock the door on life.

Presence invites it in.

And presence is nothing if not generous.

You are allowed to love your partner, your child, your dog, your friends.

You are allowed to savor your morning coffee, your warm bed, your soft routine, your favorite songs, your small pockets of joy.

You are allowed to want intimacy, connection, sex, laughter, rest, belonging.

Just don't let any of it become the ruler of your peace.

This is not a moral teaching. It's a practical one. The moment you cling, you leave the present for an imagined future where loss is already happening. And the moment you loosen, you return.

There is a simple rhythm at the heart of non-attachment — a rhythm so old the body knows it better than the mind ever will:

Hold —
don't grasp.
Let go —
don't push away.
Receive —
but do not take from.
Give —
without expectation.

109

These are not rules.

They're reminders of how it feels to be open.

When you meet life with open hands, you discover that nothing needs to be held tightly to remain meaningful.

Most things stay long enough when you stop trying to cage them.

And the ones that don't?

They were never meant to stay.

Non-attachment doesn't make life smaller.

It makes it softer.

More spacious.

More alive.

It turns enjoyment back into enjoyment
instead of turning it into fear.

6

"We never step into the same river twice, for it is not the same river and we are not the same person."

— Heraclitus

Some moments appear only once, and perhaps their beauty comes from that very fact.

I once stood before *The Allegory of Painting* in Boston. I hadn't planned the visit. I hadn't arranged my life around it. I simply happened to walk into a room on a certain day, carrying a certain version of myself. In another season, at another time, with another mind, the moment would not have met me the same way — or perhaps wouldn't have met me at all.

The painting has endured centuries of light, weather, and slow decay, but its meeting with me happened just once. Never before. Never again.

Not because the painting was temporary — though all things are.

And not because I was fixed — because I wasn't.

But because every encounter in life is a one-time alignment of countless conditions: who we are, where we are, what we're carrying, and what the world happens to be offering in that exact breath.

Impermanence gives rise to presence.

If things lasted forever, we would never bother to look.

Clinging tries to force repetition.

But presence asks only for attention.

Standing there in front of that Vermeer, I didn't need to hold it, name it, or preserve it. The moment was complete simply because I was there for it. Aum isn't only for meditation cushions. Sometimes it appears in a museum, in a quiet room, in the stillness between looking and recognizing that the looking itself is unrepeatable.

When I stop insisting that life remain as I prefer, I begin to see it as it is. And somehow, what it is becomes what I prefer.

Non-attachment does not diminish beauty.

It lets beauty be what it already is:

here briefly, then gone,

leaving the moment more luminous for its passing.

7

Everything we love changes. Everything we hold eventually leaves our hands, whether by time, circumstance, or our own growth. This isn't a disaster. It's how life moves.

Impermanence feels harsh only when we fight it. When we stop fighting, it becomes quieter. It becomes a fact instead of a threat. A simple truth: things come, things go, and something in us keeps going with them.

Daily life is full of small endings. A conversation ends. A season ends. A habit falls away. A version of ourselves shows it's finished and another one begins. Even joy concludes. Even sorrow shifts. Nothing holds its shape for long.

Non-attachment is the practice of meeting these changes without tightening. Not rushing anything away. Not dragging anything back. Just recognizing that every part of life has its moment, and its moment passes.

When the mind stops insisting that life remain exactly as it has been, a kind of ease appears. Moments become enough while they're here. They don't need to promise anything. They don't need to last.

This chapter has simply been about loosening — loosening around desire, around identity, around moments that feel special, around the idea that we can keep anything exactly as it is. Loosening makes room for something gentler to rise on its own.

And without fanfare, the loosening naturally leads toward the deeper territory that follows. Not dramatically. Not all at once. Just the way everything transitions:

quietly,

honestly,

in its own time.

The Many Deaths of Life

Live or die—two words.

Not quite my shape, even then.

I was just the going.

1

When the mind stops demanding that life remain exactly as it has been, something subtle begins to happen. A kind of ease appears around the edges. Moments feel sufficient while they're here, without requiring guarantees. They don't need to last to be meaningful. They don't need to promise a second act.

Non-attachment isn't an escape from life; it's a way of standing inside it without bracing. Once we loosen our grip, even slightly, we start to notice what was always happening beneath our attempts to hold things still:
everything is already in motion.
Every thought.

Every role.

Every version of us.

Every person we've loved.

Every moment we keep trying to preserve.

Life never stays in its original shape.

It can't.

And yet, we rarely notice this truth until we soften enough to let the world move without taking it personally.

We imagine we endure a single great ending someday — a final dissolution at the end of our lives. But the truth is quieter, and far more intimate:

we experience thousands of small endings long before the final one.

A self-image dies.

A chapter closes.

A certainty dissolves.

A relationship shifts.

A belief burns out.

An identity sheds without announcing its departure.

These are the many deaths of life — the dissolving points built into the fabric of existence. Rarely dramatic. Often unnoticed. But each one nudges us toward clarity.

And if the previous chapter was about softening the hand,

this one is about seeing what becomes visible when the hand is soft enough to let life move as it must.

2

The Buddha taught that suffering is part of the human experience. Not as a cosmic judgment, not as karma tallying up its scores — simply as the condition of living in a world where nothing stays the same.

You can verify this without believing anything spiritual:

Flowers emerge from the ground.

They bloom.

They fade.

They fall.

That cycle isn't tragic. It's sequence. Everything alive follows it, including us.

Emotions shift.

Bodies age.

Relationships evolve.

Roles end.

Certainties loosen.

Even our sense of who we are changes shape again and again.

There is nothing wrong with this. It is the natural rhythm operating at every level of existence.

But we suffer because we keep hoping for a loophole.

We want the things we love to stay in their current form.

We want roles to continue indefinitely.

We want the people we depend on to remain exactly as they are.

We want our lives to pause in the moments that feel safe or beautiful.

We want permanence in a world that doesn't offer it. And when we don't get it, we assume something has gone wrong. But nothing has gone wrong. Life is simply behaving the way life behaves.

The bent blade of grass thinks the whole garden is crooked. When our expectations are rigid, the world looks like it's failing us. When our desires harden into demands, reality feels unfair. Our inner bend becomes a lens that makes everything appear misaligned. What hurts is not the movement of life, but our attempt to keep it from moving.

Everything we love will change.

We cannot stop that from happening.

We can only decide whether to suffer the changing or make space for it.

We don't suffer because life is cruel.

We suffer because the mind refuses to let things be what they are.

3

This is what we have been working toward since the first moment we closed our eyes and noticed a single breath. How it arrives. How it fills us. How it sustains all our shifting facets. The suchness of our being. Every inhale supporting a self already in motion. Every exhale letting that self slip into the next one.

But breath has another side.

Last breaths.

Last moments.

Last words — including the ones we never got to say.

This is where the old instinct rises: the rage against the dying of the light. Not because we misunderstand death, but because the ego tightens hardest when it senses its own dissolving. It demands permanence. It demands exceptions. It demands a world that does not change simply because we are not ready for it to.

It's strange, isn't it, how we are born into families, and how those who become family are born into us. The mind files them in a category all their own — fixed, permanent, unchanging, incapable of leaving. They feel closest to our identity, woven into the core of who we believe ourselves to be. So when they pass, or drift, or transform, something inside us refuses to compute it. The world tilts. The classification system breaks. The mind can't make sense of people no longer being there.

This is where everything we've learned matters most.

All the loosening.

All the softening.

All the practice of letting life move without demanding it pause.

The strength of a tree is not the girth of its trunk, nor the spread of its branches, nor the depth of its roots. The true strength of a tree is its permission to itself to bend in the wind. Without that permission, even the mightiest would fall.

And this is our task, too:

not to become unbreakable,

but to allow ourselves to bend with the changing world instead of resisting it.

4

Everything we have practiced so far — the loosening, the noticing, the quiet moments where the inner narrator forgot to speak — was never meant for calm days. It was meant for this. For the moments that feel impossible to survive. For the losses that tear through the center of a life and leave the mind unable to reconcile what has happened.

It's easy to misunderstand meditation as preparation for serenity.

But from the very first page, we said the opposite:

Meditation does not create chaos; it reveals it.

It shows you what's inside you before you have to meet it in the world.

Those early breaths were rehearsals for the moments when quiet is no longer optional but necessary. For the moments when life reorganizes you against your will.

Loss is where every teaching lands.

When something or someone essential disappears, the mind rushes to fill the space with stories: *I can't survive this. This shouldn't have happened. I'm ruined. I'm alone. This is the end of me.* The narrator becomes frantic, loud, desperate. It tries to force permanence back into a world that has already changed.

But this is exactly where the practice begins — not by silencing grief, but by refusing to believe the narrator's catastrophes.

Because underneath the panic, the breath is still there.

And beneath the breath, space still exists.

And within that space, aum can still appear —

not as calm, not as clarity, not as peace,

but as presence.

Aum is not the absence of pain.

Aum is the absence of resistance to pain.

It is the moment you stop trying to un-happen what has already happened.

The moment where the mind, exhausted, lets the truth in.

The moment where you feel the full weight of what you've lost without adding the weight of everything you fear losing next.

Grief is not a distraction from your practice. Grief is the practice.

Those tiny moments of aum you tasted before —
the pause before sleep, the hush after laughter,
the breath where the narrator forgot its script —
they return here, not to comfort you but to keep you company.

They are the proof that even inside devastation,
awareness is still possible.
The world may feel unrecognizable,
but the sky is still above you.
The breath is still arriving.
The space inside the breath is still available.

And inside that space, something soft can begin to move: not acceptance, not closure, but permission.

Permission to feel the grief directly, without the story.

Permission to break and not believe you are broken.

Permission to hurt without deciding the hurt will last forever.

Permission to let pain be pain without letting the mind turn it into suffering.

This is how a human survives what should have destroyed them. Not by being strong in the way the world imagines strength. Not by staying rigid or fearless or untouched. But by bending — the way the tree bends — without abandoning themselves. The strength of a tree is not its trunk or its roots. Its strength is the permission it gives itself to yield when the wind rises. Grief is that wind.

Meditation taught you how to breathe inside storms.

Non-attachment taught you how to let the world move without demanding it pause.

Aum taught you how to find the place inside yourself that remains untouched.

Now all of that gathers here, in the hardest part of being alive.

You do not need to stay calm.

You do not need to be wise.

You do not need to rise above anything.

You only need to remain present enough to meet the truth of what is happening without abandoning yourself. Just as we learned to enjoy the good things without attaching and demanding they stay, so too must we grieve our losses without insisting they resolve, without trying to rush our way out of pain, without forcing the heart to be stronger than it is.

Grief asks for honesty, not control. It asks us to feel what is here, not what we wish were here. It asks us to soften around the hurt instead of tightening against it. To let the ache move, instead of letting the mind turn it into suffering.

That is what it means not to suffer your suffering. That is what makes loss survivable. That is the evolution of every chapter that came before this one.

5

We talk about the many deaths of life as if they are unusual events, rare intrusions into an otherwise stable existence. But loss does not break the pattern of life — it reveals the pattern. Every day, in ways too small to register, parts of us end. Chapters close quietly. Selves are shed without ceremony. The person you were this morning is not the one reading these words now.

Identity feels solid only because the mind prefers consistency over truth. But the "self" we carry is not a fixed object. It is a temporary arrangement of memory, habit, preference, fear, and hope. It changes shape with every new experience, every conversation, every disappointment, every moment of tenderness. What we call "me" is as fluid as everything else in nature.

Loss makes this visible.

When someone leaves our lives—through death, distance, or circumstance—we don't just lose them. We lose the version of ourselves that existed in relation to them. A parent dies, and we are no longer someone's child in the same way. A relationship ends, and the self built around that union dissolves. A dream collapses, and the self who believed in it disappears with it.

This is why grief feels like vanishing.

It is not only the world that changes shape; it is us.

Part of who we believed we were no longer exists.

Part of our identity dies.

The ego responds to this with panic. It tries to rebuild the old world, restore the old identity, resurrect the old self. It insists we go back to who we were before the loss. But no matter how hard we try, the person we were is gone. Identity doesn't return to an earlier shape any more than a flame can return to being a spark.

The many deaths of life are not failures of the self.

They are the self evolving in real time.

We grow not through stability but through dissolution.

Each small death reshapes us, widens us, deepens us.

Every version of us that disappears makes room for another to emerge.

And in the middle of these dissolutions, aum becomes more than a concept. It becomes the one place interior life remains steady. Aum is the awareness beneath the changing story of who we think we are. It is what remains when the narrator goes quiet, when identity loosens, when the old self falls away. Aum is not the self—it is what notices the self shifting.

When grief strips away who we were, aum is the thread that remains unbroken.

It is how we stay present when the mind wants to flee.

It is how we breathe when nothing feels breathable.

It is how we remember we are still here, even when parts of us are not.

Meeting the death of a self is not about strength.

It is about honesty.

It is about allowing the old identity to dissolve without forcing a new one too quickly.

It is about giving grief the space it requires without letting the mind turn that space into a story of permanent ruin.

In this way, we learn to let the small deaths happen.

We stop fighting life's natural rhythm.

We let identities end when their time is over.

We let roles fade.

We let the self shed and re-form.

We let the world move, and we move with it.

You have died a thousand times already. Every version of you that no longer exists is proof that you have survived every ending so far. The many deaths of life have shaped you, undone you, rebuilt you. And each time, you have come back changed, but still whole.

This is the quiet truth at the center of all the teachings: you are not defined by the selves you lose, but by the awareness that remains through every loss. As Philip Roth wrote, "Nothing lasts and yet nothing passes either, and nothing passes just because nothing lasts."

Only Room for Love

They fly, yet remain—

the birds and their endless sky.

I enter like them.

1

By the time you arrive here, aum is no longer a concept you're trying to understand. You've already felt it in fleeting, unmistakable moments: the breath that arrives before a thought forms, the quiet between emotions, the small pause where awareness stands without needing permission. Aum was never meant to be mastered. It was meant to be recognized and noticed the way you might notice the warmth of your own hands after forgetting they were touching.

Everything you've read was a gradual return to something your mind has always known but rarely acknowledged: you can meet your life as it unfolds without demanding it remain as you prefer. The mind creates weather — thoughts, reactions, memories, fears — but awareness is the sky that holds all of it without strain. Through joy, disappointment, change, and loss, something in you has remained intact. Not untouched, but unbroken.

Meditation served only as the doorway to this understanding. It didn't create peace; it simply revealed the layers of tension you've been carrying. Beneath that tension, it revealed the quiet you've always had access to. The Western mind loves measurement, improvement, and mastery, but presence answers to none of these. It responds to the willingness to stop interfering with the moment long enough to actually inhabit it.

More than anything, this journey has been about loosening. Loosening the grip around the self, loosening around expectations, loosening around the idea that life must cooperate with your preferences. Loosening makes room for gentleness, curiosity, and the kind of strength that does not depend on control. It allows you to respond to life rather than brace against it.

None of this asks you to transcend being human. It asks you to be human with less resistance. To feel without drowning. To think without believing every thought. To allow endings without assuming they erase you. To enjoy what's good without clutching it for dear life. Feel what's real. Weep what's heavy. Move right on. The rhythm of aum has never been about removing the texture of your days. It has been about giving you the space to experience all of it without abandoning yourself.

And when love becomes confusing or uneven — when you're not sure how to give it or whether you deserve it —

return to something simple: be the scale by which love is measured. Let your own steadiness set the tone. Love costs nothing to offer, yet its value is immeasurable. Love unjustly.

To give unjust love is to release love with no ledger, no expectation of its return, and no deciding the recipient. It's the open palm instead of the clenched fist. It's loving with a kind of holy indifference — not coldness, but freedom — letting the warmth go where it goes, find who it finds, change what it changes. Like the dandelion that never once demands its seeds come back home. She simply yields them to the wind, knowing her only role is to offer, not to control where they land.

2

Everything here returns to one truth: you can come back to yourself at any moment. Aum is not escape. It is re-entry, steady and honest.

Be here. Be present, and presently becoming. The journey never left its beginning. You simply learned to see it from the distance where meaning appears.

This is not a conclusion. Awareness is the continuation you carry with you into whatever comes next.

I may be nearly beginning.
I may be nearly ending —
but either way I am amused.

Appendix

Crafting Your Aum Practice
A practical guide for awareness in an ordinary, overwhelming world.

I. The Ordinary Sacred

Aum isn't found in rare moments — it shows up in the small movements you repeat every day.
Brushing your teeth.
Tying your shoes.
Rinsing a cup.
Folding laundry.
Unlocking the front door.
When you give even one of these actions your full attention, the moment steadies.
You stop rehearsing or anticipating.
You're simply here.

Awareness doesn't demand special conditions.
It asks only for your presence.

II. Staying Awake in a Loud World

Life pulls at you from every direction.
 Aum doesn't remove the noise — it helps you stay yourself inside it.
Clarity instead of withdrawal.
 Boundaries are honest limits, not apologies.
Responding instead of reacting.
 Take one breath before you speak.
 One unforced breath interrupts a hundred thoughts.
Stability in conflict.
 Feel your posture: spine, shoulders, jaw, feet.
 A steady body keeps you present when emotions surge.
Overstimulation
 Narrow your focus to a single sensation — hands, breath, contact.
 The moment becomes manageable again.
Emotional flooding
 Pay attention to the sensation itself rather than the explanation you want to give it.
Meditation as structure, not escape
 Awareness isn't meant to distance you from life — it's meant to keep you in it without losing yourself.

III. Simple Structures That Hold a Practice

Aum becomes real when you weave it into things you already do.

Micro-aums
 Take a few seconds to observe one breath or one sensation.
 Short moments done often change more than long sessions done rarely.

Anchor rituals
 A brief cue in the morning and another in the evening.
 Consistency matters more than length.

Event-based aums
 Attach awareness to everyday actions — opening a door, washing your hands, buckling your seatbelt.

The rule of returning
 You will drift.
 Everyone drifts.
 Noticing you drifted is the moment you return.
 Beginning again is the entire practice.

IV. Morning and Evening Rituals

Morning
 • Notice your first breath. You are here before the narrator arrives.

• At the mirror, catch the quiet before self-talk begins.

• Take a steady inhale and exhale before walking out the door.

Evening

• Set your phone down deliberately, not as collapse.

• Let your shoulders soften; allow the day to settle.

• Your final breath before sleep is a small letting-go — a reminder that something in you continues through every ending.

These openings and closings frame the day.

V. Aum Practice Patterns

Reliable ways to return to awareness in any situation.

1. The One-Breath Interrupt

Use a single inhale and exhale to interrupt momentum — thoughts, emotions, reactions.

One breath can shift your entire direction without force.

2. Sensation Before Story

When something hits you, feel the physical sensation first.
Sensation is real.

The story usually isn't.

3. Presence in Transitions

Every shift — waking, sitting, standing, entering a room — is a natural moment to return to yourself.

You don't need to add anything; simply notice the change.

4. *The Pause Reset*

Before responding, pause for half a second.
 That small opening is where clear decisions come from.
 It doesn't make you slow — it makes you steady.

5. *Beauty as a Pace-Setter*

Let one simple thing — a color, a sound, a gesture — slow you down.
 When beauty lands, hold nothing hostage.

6. *Letting Emotions Move*

Feelings are temporary.
 Your awareness is not.
 Let emotions rise and fall without turning them into identity.

7. *Returning Without Punishment*

The moment you notice you've drifted, you've already returned.
 No judgment required.

VI. Aum in Daily Practices

Walking
 Use each step as an anchor: step → awareness → step.

Conversation
 Pause before speaking.
 Your tone changes when you're present.

Eating

Let the first bite land fully — flavor, texture, temperature.

Driving

Notice your hands on the wheel or the weight of your body in the seat.
Awareness reduces tension without changing the situation.

Household Tasks

Treat simple chores as built-in opportunities for presence.
Repetition steadies the mind.

Physical Intimacy

Intimacy deepens when both people place their attention in the same moment.
Stay with the connection instead of evaluating yourself.

VII. Life Applications: Work, Home, Kids, Pets

Environmental Design

Choose lighting and spaces that help you slow down.
Keep one object you find grounding where you frequently pass.

Work

Take a breath before replying.
Pause between tasks.

Check your posture when stress rises.

Kids

Match their present-moment awareness when possible.
Use small transitions as shared resets.

Pets

Animals don't leave the moment.
Let their pace recalibrate yours.

VIII. Troubleshooting the Practice

What to do when things get difficult.

Thoughts and Mental Noise

"My mind is too loud."
Awareness doesn't silence thought — it keeps you from
getting swept up in it.

"I overthink everything."
Thinking is natural; believing every thought isn't.
Notice when you've wandered and return gently.

"I get stuck in loops."
Shift attention to physical sensation.
Your body breaks cycles your mind can't.

"I can't focus."
You don't need focus.
You need to return.

"My mind races at night."
Settle your attention into your body: weight, breath, contact.

Emotions and Overwhelm

"I get overwhelmed easily."
Shrink the moment to one sensation you can actually feel.

"My emotions take over."
Feel the sensation of the emotion before narrating it.

"I shut down."
Notice the shutdown itself — it's still a signal, not a failure.

"I don't process feelings well."
You don't need to "solve" them.
You need to stay with them long enough for them to change on their own.

"I feel numb."
Numbness means you've hit capacity.
Approach it gently.

Body and Physical Tension

"I'm always tense."
Meet the tension with awareness, not force.
Let presence do the softening.

"I'm not grounded."
Return to contact: feet on the floor, hands on something stable.

"I forget to breathe."
Your body breathes automatically.
Aum simply asks you to notice.

"I dissociate."
Name one sensation you can actually feel right now.

Relationships and Social Triggers

"I react too quickly."
Take one breath.
It isn't hesitation — it's clarity.

"I shut down in conflict."
Adjust your posture.
A steadier body helps you stay emotionally engaged.

"I lose myself around certain people."
Notice your baseline — breath, tone, pace — and return to it often.

"I can't handle criticism."
Feel where it lands in your body before judging the words.
Most of the sting is physical.

Habits, Consistency, and Discipline

"I forget to practice."
Noticing you forgot means you just practiced.

"I'm inconsistent."
Everyone is.
Consistency grows when the practice feels like relief, not obligation.

"I drift constantly."
Drifting is human.
Returning is intentional.

"I feel lazy."
Awareness requires far less effort than avoidance.
Start with five seconds.

"Life gets busy and I stop."
Tie aum to one action you already do every day.

Identity and Self-Perception

"I don't feel spiritual."
Good — aum isn't about belief.
It's about noticing what's already happening.

"I'm doing it wrong."
If you noticed anything, you did it right.

"I don't know who I am when I'm present."
Awareness comes before identity.
It's normal to feel open or unfamiliar.

"I don't trust myself."
Presence rebuilds trust through clarity, not pressure.

"I feel unworthy."
Worth is something you remember, not something you earn.

Body Image

"I hate how I look."
Your body is an experience, not an object.

"I'm uncomfortable in my body."
Start with neutral sensations — temperature, breath,
contact.

"I compare myself constantly."
Comparison is a story.
You can choose whether to participate.

"I want to change but feel ashamed."
You can improve something without despising it.

Addiction, Compulsion, Overuse

"I keep doing things I know aren't good for me."
Compulsion is your nervous system trying to regulate, not
a moral failing.

"Food/alcohol/screens feel out of control."
Notice the urge itself — not just the behavior.
Space gives you choice.

"I binge to numb out."
Numbing is a sign you're overloaded.
Awareness lowers the intensity enough to breathe again.

"I feel ashamed of my habits."
Shame keeps the cycle going.
Awareness interrupts it.

Intimacy and Connection

"I'm afraid of being seen."
Let yourself feel the fear before acting from it.

"I disconnect during sex."
Return to breath or contact.
Presence reconnects more reliably than performance.

"I want deeper intimacy."
Deeper intimacy grows when attention becomes shared,
not when roles are performed.
Stay with what you're feeling, not with how you think
you're doing.

"I feel unlovable."
That is a thought, not a truth.
Be the scale by which love is measured.

Setback and Failure

"I messed up today."
Begin again.

"I lost my temper."
Awareness can arrive late and still matter.

"I regressed."
Progress isn't linear.
It moves like a pulse.

"I avoided everything."
Avoidance means you've exceeded capacity.
Start with one small action.

"I gave up."
You paused.
Now return.

Mortality, Loss, Fragility

"I'm afraid of death."
Fear of death is part of being human.
Your mind imagines endings it can't comprehend — it's doing its job.
Aum doesn't ask you to erase the fear.
It brings you back to what's actually happening now: this breath, this moment.
The fear loosens when you stop feeding imagined futures.

"I fear losing people."
Loss is inevitable.
Abandoning yourself during loss is not.

"I feel fragile."
Fragility isn't failure — it's your system asking for a slower pace.

IX. When You Fall Off

You will drift.
You will forget.
You will get swept up.
None of this ruins the practice.
The moment you notice is the moment you return.
No judgment.
No reset required.
Just come back.

X. The Thread That Ties It Together

Aum isn't calm, perfection, or mastery.
 It's the awareness in which everything happens.
You don't need a different life to practice.
 You only need to notice the one you already have.
Returning is always possible.
 That is aum.

About the Author

Craig Reuter is a contemplative writer and long-time meditation practitioner whose work explores the architecture of awareness and the subtle shift between thinking and noticing. Drawing from meditation, evolutionary psychology, and the lived experience of unraveling his own Western conditioning, he approaches philosophy with clarity, humility, and a quiet sense of humor.

When he's not writing, Craig works in clinical analytics and can often be found practicing yoga, exploring breathwork, or attempting to make sense of the strange, beautiful mess of being human.

He lives on Long Island with Prudence, his endlessly spoiled King Charles Cavalier and the closest thing he has to a spiritual teacher. She remains blissfully unaware that half the insights in this book are her fault.